W9-BLI-158

The
New World Disorder

—— The ——
New World Disorder

Reflections of a European

—— by Tzvetan Todorov ——
Preface by Stanley Hoffmann

Translated by Andrew Brown

polity

Copyright © this translation Polity Press 2005

"The New World Disorder" was first published under the title "Le Nouveau Désordre mondial" by Éditions Robert Laffont in Paris.
© 2003 by Editions Robert Laffout/Susanna Lea Associates

Liberté • Égalité • Fraternité
RÉPUBLIQUE FRANÇAISE

This book is supported by the French Ministry for Foreign Affairs, as part of the Burgess programme headed for the French Embassy in London by the Institut Français du Royaume-Uni.

The right of Tzvetan Todorov to be identified as Author of this Work has been asserted in accordance with the UK Copyright, Designs and Patents Act 1988.

First published in 2005 by Polity Press

Polity Press
65 Bridge Street
Cambridge CB2 1UR, UK.

Polity Press
350 Main Street
Malden, MA02148, USA

All rights reserved. Except for the quotation of short passages for the purpose of criticism and review, no part of this publication may be reproduced, stored in a retrieval system, or transmitted, in any form or by any means, electronic, mechanical, photocopying, recording or otherwise, without the prior permission of the publisher.

ISBN 0 7456 3368 4
ISBN 0 7456 3369 2 (paperback)

A catalogue record for this book is available from the British Library

Typeset in 11 on 13pt Sabon
by Graphicraft Ltd, Hong Kong
Printed and bound in Great Britain by MPG Books Ltd, Bodmin, Cornwall

For further information on Polity, visit our website: www.polity.co.uk

Contents

Preface

Few texts devoted to recent international events, the war on Iraq and its implications, and the necessary European responses to American neo-imperialism, have seemed to me as profound and trenchant as this foray, on the part of one of the greatest intellectuals of our time, into the domain of international relations. Tzvetan Todorov, that Renaissance (or Enlightenment) Man, who has, with an exceptional power of insight and concentration, shed light on so many subjects – from linguistics to totalitarianism, from the history of ideas to philosophy and anthropology – here gives us an exemplary lesson. He explains what the foreign policy of a liberal democracy ought to be in the contemporary world; he warns us against the temptations of omnipotence and the unilateral resort to force; he argues for pluralism and against messianism – against the delusion that we can export democracy. He does this in a style worthy of Montesquieu and de Tocqueville, in the tradition of a way of thinking that concurs with Camus, for whom the means employed are just as important as the avowed ends. He alerts us to the danger of a power that is not controlled from within and not contained from without, and he thus develops a critique of the new global strategy of the United States that is much more convincing than the current angry denunciations and prejudices.

In addition, he gives us a method by which we can limit, or soften, the inevitable supremacy of the American "hyper-power": a Europe that would not be merely an example of the reconciliation of nations that had been for so long in conflict in a continent torn apart by war, and a model of peaceful and prosperous unification, but one which could also become what he calls a "tranquil power." This Europe ought to be capable of reducing its dependence on the United States in the domain of defense, and of assuming its responsibilities in the field of foreign policy. This should enable it to gain a hearing in an America tempted to resort to force wherever necessary – a temptation based on a conception both casual and contemptuous of alliances, and of international law and organizations. Finally, he puts forward some ideas that are convincing, ambitious, and original, on the need to adapt European institutions and on the values which the European Union can and must defend and promote in a dangerous and chaotic world.

So much in so few pages! As a European who for almost half a century has been transplanted to the United States, I am proud to have the privilege and the honor of prefacing this work by a man whose wisdom and erudition have long dazzled me and whose ideas as developed in this book I essentially share.

Stanley Hoffmann
Harvard University

Translator's Note

Although the French version of this book is barely a year old, events have obviously overtaken it here and there: the enlargement of the EU has now taken place, and a European country, Spain, has been the target of a terrorist attack. I have not drawn attention to the occasional moments at which Todorov's remarks would need to be updated, since the unpredictability of history is obviously one of his themes.

Introduction

Rarely has an event that happened far away from our towns and countryside generated as much passion and debate as the conflict between the United States and Iraq in the first half of 2003. The battles did not take place on the soil of our continent, and yet all Europeans felt involved, as if they had the impression that it was their fate too that was being decided. I have rarely read as many newspapers and heard as many declarations, and I was far from being the only one. The debate was all the more lively in that the viewpoints were irreconcilable, even though they were based on an appeal to the same ideals: the democratic order, human rights. A major proportion of the European population seemed torn between two quite distinct attitudes: either condemning the war or condemning the dictatorship of Saddam Hussein – whereas the effect of the war was in fact the end of the dictatorship. Could one support both positions simultaneously, without contradicting oneself? Was it necessary to abandon one of the two positions – and if so, which one?

That's not all. The conflict, and the debates to which it gave rise, also threw into question the identity of Europe. Negotiations on European institutions are normally of

interest only to experts or a handful of politicians dedi-
cated to that cause; inquiries into the nature of European
civilization and society at best fuel discussions between
academics. Now here we saw, all at once, under the pressure of events – the war! – European identity becoming
the object of a shared debate, which was also relayed by
all the media. There was, indeed, matter for concern:
for the first time since 1945, it seemed that Europe no
longer wished to follow the political line taken by the
United States. Or rather, on this military question, certain
European governments were opposed to others. Old rifts
re-emerged, and new ones developed: there was disagree-
ment between "Atlanticists" and "Europeans", between
the "old" and the "new" Europe. And, at least in certain
countries, there was an additional split between public
opinion and government policy. All of these divisions led
Europeans to examine the basic question: how can the
identity of Europe be described? And what kind of Europe
do we want to see in the future?

The liveliness of these debates forced me to leave behind
my usual occupations as a historian of ideas and cultures;
I felt the need to see more clearly into the events that had
just occurred and to bring a little order into my own reactions as a citizen – hence the following pages. Doubtless,
my personal links and loyalties also motivate my interest
in this topic. Born and brought up in one part of Europe –
Bulgaria – I have been living for 40 years now in another
– France. The distance between the two did not merely
separate East from West, but also Communist totalitarianism and democracy. It was with joy that I witnessed, from
the western side, the fall of the Berlin Wall, and with deep
satisfaction that I saw the first steps towards European
reunification: now I could consider myself to be a member
of Europe as a whole. In sensibility, I find myself close
both to Eastern Europe and to Western Europe. At the
same time, the United States is hardly a foreign country
to me: I've visited it many times, I've lived there, and I
have friends and relatives there. In short, the new tensions

within and without Europe are tensions that I experience inside myself. This is doubtless why, today, I have chosen to assume my responsibilities as a twenty-first-century European and give them expression.

— 1 —

The Reasons for the War

Such different reasons have been put forward for the war between the United States and Iraq, depending on the group to which one belonged, that a certain confusion inevitably developed in people's minds. Let us examine, to begin with, the main answers to the question "Why did this war happen?". On this basis we will be able to judge its legitimacy.

In his speech to the nation on 17 March 2003, which amounted to a declaration of war, President George W. Bush had put forward a twofold reason. "The Iraqi regime continues to possess and conceal some of the most lethal weapons ever devised [...] it has aided, trained and harboured terrorists, including operations of Al Qaeda."[1] It was the combination of the two which constituted the threat: Iraq produced weapons, it could place them at the disposal of the terrorists responsible for the attacks of 11 September. Was this threat credible?

What needs to be said straightaway is that the first assertion contains an obvious exaggeration: quite obviously, Iraq is far from being the country which has dreamt up the most deadly weapons. Bush is playing modest: this honor falls to Western countries, the United States first and foremost. But let's leave that aside; did Iraq possess such weapons in the period leading up to the war?

By "weapons of mass destruction," three types of product are meant: nuclear, biological, and chemical weapons. It is certain that Iraq did not possess the first category: after the Israeli bombing of its nuclear installations, and thanks to the constant surveillance of its territory by the Western powers, it was unable to resume its program. We have learned since the end of the war that the accusations concerning its resumption were unfounded. It is equally certain that Iraq had produced biological weapons, but here too, it is well known that these do not remain effective for long, and their production dated back several years. These weapons, if they did still exist, had become unusable. Finally, chemical weapons, which had also been manufactured by Iraq, had been destroyed following the First Gulf War in 1991. Neither before, during, or even after the military intervention, was any credible proof provided of the real existence of these weapons (I am writing these words on 19 June 2003).

On the other hand, a counter-proof *has* been provided: even if we suppose that Iraq did have such weapons, it did not use them. And yet it had every opportunity to do so: the country had been attacked, its inferiority when it came to other types of weapons was evident, its leader Saddam Hussein knew that he now had nothing to lose, and he wasn't the type to skimp on the reaction he adopted. Why, then, did he not seek to defend himself by every means available, for example by the chemical weapons at his disposal? One of the possible answers is: because he didn't have any.

Another answer is equally possible: because he didn't want to. This type of weapon is, after all, double-edged: if you use them, you also risk being subject to their effects. Now, however filled with the sense of his own strength Saddam Hussein may have been, he cannot have been unaware of the fact that the United States (or Great Britain, or Israel, etc.) had the same weapons at their disposal, in bigger quantities and of better quality; their response would have been fearsome. Using them would have been equivalent to committing suicide. In reality, these weapons can be used against someone weaker than you are, someone who doesn't possess them – such as Iran, or the Shiite or Kurdish populations within Iraq itself – but not against a superior power. But whether it was a question of *being able* to deploy them or *wanting* to do so, one thing is sure: there was no risk of such weapons being used against the United States and its allies.

The war against Islamic terrorism is based on legitimate self-defense: Western countries (among others) were attacked, and now they seek to protect themselves. But was Iraq aiding international terrorism, in particular the al-Qaeda network? Here too, no convincing proof has yet been provided. The only thing known was that the Iraqi government paid an indemnity to the families of Palestinian suicide bombers, those who sacrificed their own lives in murderous attacks. One can and should condemn the encouragement given to such actions, but we should not confuse these desperate gestures, part of a limited and very definite context as they are, with the terrorist attacks in Western countries, among them that of 11 September 2001, which were driven by purely ideological motivations.

What is more, this connection between Saddam Hussein and Osama bin Laden seemed implausible on the ideological level. The Iraqi regime was secular from the start, and for that reason had drawn down on itself the opprobrium of Islamic terrorists. The latter recruited their volunteers in other Muslim countries, first and foremost Saudi Arabia. The two could have come together only in extreme circumstances, in the face of a clear common enemy: in the case of a war against Iraq, for instance . . . It is to be doubted whether the American intervention seriously weakened terrorism.

The war on terrorism is not simple: it's a task which requires patience and tenacity. In comparison, the war against Iraq was easy – it was enough to bomb the country, and crush it under an infinitely superior power. Could this intervention really be labeled "anti-terrorist"? It's difficult to avoid the impression that this was an easy option, based on the desire to reassure public opinion at home: as usual, they looked for the key where it was easy to do so, not where they'd lost it!

The first reasons put forward – the possession of weapons of mass destruction, the link with terrorist networks – did not appear convincing, and the field was wide open to the speculations of opponents of the war, who set to work to look for the hidden reasons that could probably not be acknowledged. People wondered, for instance, if what we had here wasn't in reality a new attempt to embody triumphalist Christianity. President Bush had, after all, himself used the term "crusade" to describe his planned intervention, and at the same time informed us that he prays every day and strongly encourages his staff members to do the same. Yet it is my impression that the European, and in particular the French, public, used to a strict separation between Church and State, tends to overestimate the real role played by the religious motivation. The President may declare himself to be a Christian, but his close staff members and advisors, who play a decisive role in the direction his political activity takes, do not do likewise. No official organ of the Christian Church approved the war; on the contrary, there were numerous personalities – starting with the Pope – who condemned it and strongly opposed it. And George W. Bush himself quickly removed the word "crusade" from his speeches.

It has also been said that American policy had, throughout the whole Middle Eastern region, placed itself at the service of Israel's interests, and that the intervention in Iraq was a first step to settling the Israeli–Palestinian conflict. It's true that the line chosen by the current Israeli government seems to be benefiting from an indestructible American support, and it's a fact that highly placed presidential advisors had previously worked for the leaders of Likud. It's also true that the American regime derives a far from negligible advantage from its unconditional support for the Israeli government on the home front: any criticism of its policies can be put down to anti-Semitism, one of the most dishonoring rebukes that can be made these days in Western countries. But to imagine that the current choices made by the United States are the result of machinations on behalf of another state would be mere conspiracy theory. Even if the American administration often seems to be imitating the example of the Israeli Prime Minister, Ariel Sharon, who seeks to resolve all political problems by force, we can trust it to look after the interests of its own country first and foremost.

And what if the whole intervention had been carried out merely to seize the Iraqi oil reserves and enable American companies, led as they are by friends of those currently in power, to take advantage of them? This type of explanation has the rhetorical advantage of discrediting those in power by attributing basely material interests to them, disguised behind their high-sounding speeches. It also fits the mold of the familiar Marxist argument, in which material factors determine spiritual factors, and economics explains politics. It was frequently used by the leaders of former Communist countries to criticize the West, which they accused of pursuing its selfish interests under cover of lofty principles. And this was really rather paradoxical, since those same political leaders refuted the laws of Marxism by their own actions: they brought the economy of their countries to disaster so as to conform to political dogmas. In the present situation too, the need for oil and gain cannot explain everything. The war itself cost a great deal of money, the ensuing occupation has been ruinous, and any advantageous decrease in oil prices would be wiped out in advance by military expenditure. To be sure, the United States is a big oil consumer, and it would be to its advantage to control part of the world's reserves, but it can manage to do that without making war. Let's not forget, too, that the oil-producing countries need to sell, since they draw the essential part of their revenue from oil. The

interests of both groups converge without there being any
need to unleash a war.

Other reasons that cannot be openly acknowledged have
also been imputed to the American administration. It's a
well-known fact, for instance, that every country likes leaders who can bring it military victory. Maybe Bush invaded
Iraq to ensure he would be re-elected? It's equally well
known that the army seeks to prove its usefulness in the
eyes of political power, just as arms manufacturers wish to
show the effectiveness of their products. Maybe the war
was started as a result of their combined pressure – both
to test the existing weapons, obtain credits to dream up
new ones, and demonstrate to everyone that a big military
budget was a necessity? And on a more personal and less
conscious level, perhaps Bush Jr was seeking to prove to
his father that *he* could do a better job? Or to avenge the
affront of 11 September? All of these motivations surely
played a role. Everyone would try to profit from the war:
oil companies and specialists in reconstruction, arms manufacturers and even the presidential team aspiring to re-
election. But these hidden reasons are not enough to explain
why war was declared: a collective policy is not decided
on the basis of mere individual interests. It's better to go
back to the official explanations, which, after all, are not
produced *merely* to conceal the truth.

Over and above the allegations concerning dangerous
weapons and the connections with terrorists, the United
States President has always given a twofold justification
for his decision: he was acting in this way to bring liberty
to others and to ensure security at home. For instance,
in his programmatic speech of 26 February 2003 to the
American Enterprise Institute, he insisted at length on
the benefits that this war could bring the adversary and,
beyond that, all of its neighbors: "A liberated Iraq can
show the power of freedom to transform that vital region."[2]
At the same time, this action served the national interest,
which here consisted in ensuring that no regime consistently

hostile to the United States and capable of producing dangerous weapons could survive. The President and his advisors agree on affirming this twofold purpose: "America's cause is right and just: liberty for an oppressed people, and security for the American people."[3] Who could possibly be against such intentions? Furthermore, the two aims seem to be closely linked: "America's interests in security, and America's beliefs in liberty, both lead in the same direction."[4]

It is hardly surprising if the leaders of a country defend the national interest and, in consequence, take a close interest in security questions: they were elected to do just that. The desire to bring liberty to other nations is more unexpected. That is why the defenders of the current American policy insist on it. Robert Kagan, an influential ideologue and the author of a successful book, *Of Paradise and Power*, writes for example: "To the extent that Americans believe in power, they believe it must be a means of advancing the principles of a liberal civilization and a liberal world order."[5] Given this claim, we cannot help asking: do security at home and liberty for others always go together? And should they do so?

Let's first of all take the *de facto* question. Is it true that the desire to impose a liberal democracy on others has dominated the foreign policy of the United States, and, at the same time, that such a policy has always been in its interests? The reply to this double question is, it has to be admitted, negative. For example, in Latin America, the American government has managed to accommodate military dictatorships for many years – when it did not actually contribute to setting them up in the first place. The idea of starting a war to establish a more democratic regime in this place or that seems never to have crossed the mind of an American president in this period. Or else, in Asia, the United States keeps up the best of relations with countries that can hardly pass for incarnations of liberal democracy, such as Pakistan or Saudi Arabia. And can anyone claim that American policy towards the Palestinians is guided solely by the desire to ensure the liberty of this people, by the sole principles of liberal civilization?

The reasons for these exceptions to the rule of "liberty for others" are easy to explain: it is in no way certain that this liberty will increase the homeland security of the United States and thus serve its national interests. The peoples who express themselves freely risk, for good reasons or bad, being hostile to the United States. Let's take the example of a few states whose populations are Arab and Muslim, such as Egypt and Jordan. If the "peoples" of these countries were really to come to power and act in the name of their convictions, they would in all likelihood follow a much less pro-American policy than do their current leaders, who do not hesitate to restrict civil liberties and reinforce police powers. Isn't it rather naive to think that any people able to express itself freely would be favorable to us? What if that people supported a different ideal? If the people had been allowed to express themselves in Algeria, the country would have become an Islamic republic; if this eventuality did not come to pass, it was because the military intervened. The case of Turkey is, perhaps, not so very different. In the contemporary world, as Régis Debray remarked, the choice is often that between Islamic republics (which are hostile to the West) and secular dictatorships (which are favorable to it). Now, when one has to choose between democracy for others and security for oneself, everyone invariably chooses security.

These two objectives, security and liberty, are not in principle incompatible. But in fact, the means set in motion to attain them are often difficult to reconcile. The protection of security demands the use of force, and hence of the army; the liberty that enables the people to express its will may lead to the establishment of a liberal democracy. But the use of bombs and the liberal spirit do not go well together. Political liberalism, as we hardly need to be reminded, was born of the demand for religious tolerance.

It starts from the moment when, even if we are convinced that our religion is the best of all, we renounce the attempt to impose it on others by force. The liberal idea advocates the recognition of diversity – letting people lead their own lives. When, for security reasons, we go into other countries and impose on them a regime that is judged by us to be the best, we leave the liberal outlook and start to follow the logic of imperialism. The "liberal imperialism" spoken of by Kagan is, in the final analysis, a contradiction in terms, which deserves to occupy a place in the repertory of other expressions that imitate Orwell's Newspeak. Orwell himself would probably never have imagined that the procedure he denounced ("war is peace," "freedom is slavery") would today have so many practitioners, from the "humanitarian bombs" of Václav Havel to the "merciful war" of ex-general Jay Garner or the "universalist nationalism" of Kagan.

It's not true that the two aims always go together, nor that they should be placed on the same level. The decisive criterion is national interest and thus, in this case, homeland security. To set up liberal regimes in other countries is a good thing if it serves the first aim, bad if it makes it more difficult to attain. If the American government insists so much on highlighting the "liberation of the Iraqi people," this is because, in everyone's opinion, the language of virtue is superior to that of force. The Soviet Empire was well aware of this: it always declared it was fighting for the liberty of the oppressed and for peace between the nations. Noble ideals are a powerful rhetorical weapon, and even the head of the world's most powerful army cannot allow himself to ignore them. They inspire the troops, disarm the enemy's resistance, and earn the respect of third parties.

Now, the affirmation of these ideals is not necessarily pure hypocrisy. Saddam Hussein's regime was indeed a hateful dictatorship, and today its fall is regretted by no one: in this precise case, there was no conflict between security for oneself and liberty for others. It's just that if we want to debate the principles governing our policy, it's better to call a spade a spade and get our priorities right, rather than be intoxicated by fine words. The defense of security and national interests is not in the slightest dishonorable; when it can coincide with promoting liberal regimes in other countries, so much the better. What characterizes current American policy is not the mere adoption of these aims and objectives, but rather the means considered legitimate to attain them: a military intervention not based solely on legitimate defense – what has been called a "preventive war."

– 2 –

The Neo-fundamentalists

So it remains unproven that the foreign policy of the United States is always guided by the democratic ideal. But it is sometimes, and this argument has great persuasive force. Shouldn't we admire and support a country that declares it is working to overthrow tyrants, establish democracy, and defend human rights?

The ideologues of the American state have often affirmed that their country – the equivalent of the "Chosen People" in the Bible – had a vocation to impose the Good throughout the world. George Kennan, the inventor of the policy of "containment" towards the USSR, spoke of "accepting the responsibilities of moral and political leadership that history plainly intended them [the US] to bear."[1] History has here taken over God's role: it is seen as capable of plans and intentions. By what sign does history reveal them? By granting to the United States a power greater than that of other countries: might here becomes imperceptibly transformed into right.

In the official document made public by the White House on 20 September 2002, *The National Security Strategy*, President Bush made the present nature of this "election" perfectly explicit: "Today, humanity holds in its hands the opportunity to further freedom's triumph over all these foes. The United States welcomes our responsibility to lead in this great mission."[2] But the conclusions he draws from this are quite new: America needs to move from defense to attack. "We will promote [. . .] human dignity [. . .] freedom of worship and conscience." The promotion of such a lofty aim justifies resorting to any means whatsoever, in particular war.

To what kind of thinking does this political project belong? It is often claimed that George W. Bush's program, or in any case this part of his program, has been thought out by a group of neo-conservatives. But the term "conservative" is not at all a suitable label, as one of them in fact remarked. "There are almost no European-style conservatives in the United States, people who want to defend a status quo based on hierarchy, tradition, and a pessimistic view of human nature," wrote Francis Fukuyama.[3] These thinkers believe in the possibility of a radical improvement of man and society, and they are actively committed to furthering this end. But in this case they do not deserve the term "conservatives" – either neoconservatives or, as it were, old-style conservatives. A better term for them would "neo-fundamentalists": they are fundamentalists because they believe in an Absolute Good which they wish to impose on everyone; neobecause this Good is constituted, no longer by God, but by the values of liberal democracy.

Neither of these two ingredients is really new; but the combination of the two is quite unprecedented. Fundamentalists believe in absolute values: they thus reject the prevailing relativism, the excuses made for the infringements of democracy by multiculturalists, the jargon of the "politically correct." However, not being conservatives, they wish to propagate their ideal through the world by force. From this point of view, they tend to refer more frequently to the spirit of "permanent revolution." The origins of this aspect of their thinking can be found in the anti-Stalinist revolutionary Left; Daniel Cohn-Bendit is

thus both right and wrong to label these ideologues "Bol-
sheviks." Critical of the Bolshevik or Stalinist ideal, they
have preserved the mind-set of the activists: the world needs
to be made over, its problems must be resolved once and
for all, if necessary by armed force; liberty must triumph.
It's no coincidence if they include among their numbers,
both in the United States and in France, several former
Trotskyists or Maoists: the same interventionist spirit which
refuses to resign itself to the imperfections of this world
raises its head here and there – the same attraction to
violence and internationalist action.

The exporting of the Communist Revolution in the twentieth century, supported if necessary by the Red Army,
was the previous embodiment of this mind-set – but it's
true that the ideal being promoted was different. It was
not, however, the first such embodiment. In the nineteenth
century, it was the European powers, such as France and
Great Britain, which engaged in colonial wars justified by
the idea that it was necessary to bring the Good to everyone. This Good was then the equivalent of what was called
"civilization"; it was in its name that the colonizers established their domination of the countries of Africa and Asia.
Even earlier, the regiments of Napoleon had spread the
ideas of the French Revolution – liberty, equality, frater-
nity – on the point of their bayonets. The ideal, and the
power needed to realize it, were, in every case, mutually
supportive.

In an even earlier tradition, this combination was the
basis of the theologico-political order. These two elements
were inextricably linked: royalty found its legitimation in
divine right, and religious law lay at the foundation of
human law. In Christian doctrine, it was in particular certain messianic and millenarian heresies that announced the
imminent arrival of paradise on earth and declared that all
means were justified in accelerating this process. The Communist utopias were the heirs of these millenarian move-
ments, whose final objective they transformed. The same
is true of the current upsurge of millenarian activity: what

these people aspire to impose is not life in Christ but a set of values, incarnated by the United States, that amount to a variant of liberal democracy.

So the thinking behind this aspect of American foreign policy is not conservative, any more than it is liberal (since it imposes unity instead of allowing diversity to be preserved). Can we say that it's democratic? In the past, democracies resorted to it, since countries such as Great Britain and France put this ideology into practice in their colonial campaigns. The presence of this way of thinking is thus perfectly possible in a democracy, but can the two be harmoniously combined? The truth of the matter is that the democratic idea has only been able to affirm itself insofar as the unity of the theological and the political spheres was starting to fall apart. This split, demanded by the philosophers of the Renaissance and the seventeenth century, found concrete expression in the creation of the first democracies, American and French, before leading finally to the definitive separation of Church and State. What is the meaning of this split? A particular individual may think that he is leading a much more admirable life than his neighbor; yet, in a democracy, he has no right to impose his own way of life on others by force. The State ensures peace between citizens, fixes a lower limit that must not be transgressed (where a crime or an offence is committed), but does not formulate an ideal that all would be constrained to embrace. In this sense, democracy is not a "virtuous" political state.

This separation can also be found in international life, even if it appears in a different guise. A certain population may think that its God is superior to its neighbor's, and that it, rather than its neighbor, thus possesses the Supreme Good; nonetheless, it abandons the idea of declaring war on its neighbor to impose this Good on it. Democracy means that each people is sovereign, that it also has the right to define the Good for itself, rather than seeing it being imposed from outside. In consequence, when Western powers conduct their colonial wars in the name of the democracy which they claim to embody, the means used cancel out the aim pursued. How can one "promote the human dignity" of others if they are not allowed to decide on their own destiny? If we *impose* liberty on others, we subject them; if we *impose* equality on them, we judge them to be inferior.

The ideal of liberal democracy, for its part, must not be confused with that of conservatism. It's true that, insofar as it does not set itself the aim of building paradise here and now, or of ensuring the definitive triumph of liberty over its enemies foes, liberal democracy declines to sacrifice the present to the future, to further the cause of abstractions to the detriment of individuals, to justify individual deaths by the noble objectives they purportedly serve (those "humanitarian bombs," not to mention "collateral damage"). But neither does its ideal consist in resigning itself to the world as it is, and contenting itself with contemplating it in serenity. It in turn is opposed to tyrants, but seeks to combat them by means other than those of the neo-fundamentalists: by denouncing them in public, refusing to acknowledge the legitimacy of their governments, ostracizing their country from other nations, and adopting all sorts of diplomatic, political, or economic pressures.

This choice – negotiation rather than intervention, containment rather than occupation of the enemy territory – has its disadvantages: its results take longer, and they do not hold out any certain reward of a heroic halo for those who embark on it. And yet, from the democratic point of view, when the same end can be reached by two means – rapidly by violence or slowly without it – slowness is preferable. It is better to disarm Iraq in four months without killing anyone than to disarm it in four weeks while killing thousands of people.

This was the way in which the Western countries proceeded in previous decades, in the case of regimes that they condemned, such as South Africa or the Soviet Union. How did the American government contribute to the fall of the latter? Reagan did not modify the policy of containment towards the "Evil Empire," he merely added the element of an arms race which eventually revealed the structural weakness of the Communist state. He thus won the victory without firing a single shot.

The tactic of declaring war on all tyrants and all forms of injustice needs to be questioned, not only because it is impossible to realize (it would be a superhuman task), or because it would impose a permanent state of war and thereby contribute to reinforcing all the armies and all the police forces in the world (a paradoxical result of the struggle for liberty). The great Russian writer Vasilii Grossman, a remarkable analyst of twentieth-century totalitarianism, put it like this: "Whenever we see the dawn of an eternal good [. . .], the blood of old people and children is always shed."[4] Why do we need to give up the idea of imposing the Good by force? Because there is too great a risk that more suffering than joy will result: a noble end does not justify ignoble means. The victims of the temptation to do good are infinitely more numerous than those of the temptation to do evil. This is why Grossman recommended that we cultivate goodness and kindness rather than the Good, and pay more heed to individuals than to abstractions; and from this point of view, "democracy," "liberty," and "prosperity" are hardly any better than "revolution," "communism," and "classless society." Admirable ideals are not enough to ensure the happiness of humankind: while these ideals are being promoted, "the blood of old people and children is shed."

The policies of a liberal democracy at home and abroad do not take the same forms. Within a country, the state can resort to constraint (policing) to protect its power or ensure the rule of justice. When it comes to relations between states, it does not renounce the use of force; but it uses it to ensure its own sacrosanct interests, to protect its citizens and their property, not to impose an ideal order on everyone. This is the difference between democracies and totalitarian states (or other incarnations of the unity of the political and theological spheres): the former use their armed forces in legitimate self-defense, the latter use them to change the rest of the world. To fight for someone else's perfection – rather than one's own – has no part in a democratic code of ethics. The comparison of contemporary wars with that fought against Nazi Germany or Japan is invalid for the same reason: those two counties had attacked others, who were perfectly entitled to take up arms to defend themselves. The fact that the United States, after its victory over Germany and Japan, helped to set up democracy in those countries, is all to its credit; but it had not embarked on war for that reason.

This is why the recently popularized idea of the "right to interfere" is also incompatible with the democratic spirit. The war with Iraq would, on this account, be directly comparable to the intervention in Kosovo, when this expression first appeared in military rhetoric. The only difference between the two is that in Yugoslavia, in 1999, those intervening were content with taking one province out of the control of the central government without requiring that the latter be toppled; in Iraq in 2003, on the other hand, the overthrow of the government was demanded. The "right to interfere" would like to derive its authority from an appeal to democracy – but it does so at the cost of an unacceptable shift in meaning. To begin with, the "interference" at issue was humanitarian. To seize the initiative by aiding the wounded and the needy of a foreign country in no way threatens national sovereignty. The second step was claiming that those involved in the humanitarian intervention needed military protection. And finally came the third step – one which contradicted the spirit of the original initiative: the military attack was justified by the deplorable situation when it came to the humanitarian level, and people acted as if the main effect of the war was to ensure respect for human rights. In this way they ended up with that prize exhibit of Newspeak, the "humanitarian war."

Does this mean that, once one has adopted the democratic viewpoint, military intervention is justified *only* in the case of legitimate defense? No; it is also justified in the extreme case of genocide, not because of any imaginary and self-claimed right to interfere, but because of the duty of humanity. Here, quantity is transformed into quality: when a group constitutive of humanity is *exterminated*, we are all concerned, even if we are not part of that group. However, not every infraction of human rights is – fortunately – a case of genocide; nor is every tyrant a Hitler. It's better to lay the specter of the Nazi dictator to rest, and not fall back on comparisons that are misleading rather than enlightening. The law of the excluded middle doesn't rule in the political domain, and non-military action remains possible: democracies are not really obliged to choose between Munich (cowardly capitulation) and Dresden (murderous bombing).

— 3 —

The Fragility of the Empire

The justification of the war by the desire to impose democracy is no justification at all: inadequate in itself, this argument is also, as often as not, deliberately misleading: behind it we can make out a more traditional motive – national interests. But these should in no way be considered shameful, since it is the first duty of any government to defend such interests. The foreign policy of the United States is no exception in this respect; but it also has two more specific characteristics. First, this country considers that its interests are at stake over the entire surface of the globe; and secondly, it is ready to defend them by making immediate use of military force. The combination of these two features leads people to make the frequent assertion that the foreign policy of the United States is an imperial policy.

The adjective "imperialist" has for long been considered an insult, and no one wants it applied to their own cause. As Raymond Aron remarked in a study published in 1959, only *others* are described in this way. "Imperialism is the name given to the diplomacy of a great power by its rival or its spectators."[1] The power in question, on the other hand, will always try to deny that it belongs in this reviled

category: but such a denial, in turn, cannot allay all suspicion. "The sublimity of one's language is not enough to
guarantee that right will prevail," Aron continues: "rather,
it ensures that what will prevail is hypocrisy. Henceforth,
imperialists appear only in disguise and they give the name
'liberation' to what men in other centuries would have
called 'oppression'."

Whether or not the term "imperialist" applies, United
States policy is undeniably imperial, because of the avowed
presence of the two aforementioned features. But not all
imperial policies are alike. The French or British colonial-
ism of the nineteenth century was an example of one variant, establishing as it did an explicit hierarchy between
metropolis and colony; the annexationist policy of the
USSR, in the twentieth century, which consisted in inte-
grating new territories into the initial state, embodied a
different form. The American empire resembles neither of
these types, since the United States neither occupies foreign countries nor seeks to annex them; the US is content
with demanding that the governments of those countries
not be hostile on either the political or the economic level.
The term "hegemony" is perhaps the one best suited to
this kind of imperial strategy.

When was this choice first made? Every great country
seeks to extend the radius of its influence, and the United
States has been a great country ever since it was founded.
However, several more recent events have contributed to
reinforcing its role and reserving an exceptional place for
it among other great powers. The first step was taken
during the Second World War, when the former Western
powers – Germany, France, Great Britain – found themselves excluded from the competition and kept at a distance by the United States. The next rung on the ladder
was reached when the rival empire – that of the Soviet
Union – fell apart. Not only did this leave the United States
without any adversary of its own caliber, but in addition,
a few years after the fall of the Berlin Wall, the United
States decided to abandon any attempt to pick up, so to

speak, the dividends of peace: it did not take advantage of the absence of an arms race to enjoy its wealth without further delay. Quite the contrary: under the presidency of Clinton, the army budget practically doubled, with the result that American military power can no longer be matched by anyone.

The third and final stage towards what certain people call "hyperpower" status was attained following the terrorist attacks of 11 September 2001. Until then, the United States could imagine that its military superiority alone sufficed to inspire respect, and that no one would be brave enough to attack it. The US had not really taken into account the danger represented by individual terrorists ready to sacrifice themselves: having renounced their own lives, they have nothing left to lose, and there is no retaliation they need fear. This discovery of its own vulnerability led the United States to add a new chapter to its military strategy, that of "preventive war," which in its view is alone capable of preventing terrorist attacks. The war in Iraq was the direct result of this decision.

The new doctrine was codified by the document *The National Security Strategy* of 20 September 2002, which affirms that, even if the time and place of the future enemy attack are uncertain, the United States is quite within its rights to strike at those potential enemies, terrorists or states favorable to anti-American terrorism. The introduction of this notion of preventive war was a real innovation in modern international life: even if the great powers had never abstained from intervening in the lives of small states, they had never raised it to a principle that they could take the unilateral decision to start a war because of a merely possible attack. American Senator Robert Byrd was thus right to speak in this regard of a "turning point in US foreign policy," with a "radical new twist on the traditional idea of self-defense" and a revolutionary doctrine of prevention.[2]

A policy based on nothing but superior strength might be judged to be immoral. But moral judgments have no place here. Politics is not the same as morality, and must be judged by its own criteria. The real question the American government must ask itself is this: is the pursuit of global hegemony by the aid of preventive wars the best means of ensuring our security and defending our interests? Does peace through empire establish the most stable international order possible, and the one most favorable to the United States? The armed intervention against Iraq in 2003, the first major example of this strategy, allows us to observe the consequences of war outside the cabinet rooms of the experts, in the real world: and it is not very wise to praise or condemn a doctrine on the basis of merely anticipated results.

Did this war bring about the desired results? The declared objective, as we have seen, was the toppling of the dictatorship and the establishment of democracy. The first part of the program was accomplished swiftly, to the joy of Iraqi political exiles and a large part of that country's population. The second part was more complex. It has to be said that, right from the start, there was something naive about this plan, since it considered Iraqi society as an unstructured entity into which it was permissible to introduce a new political regime just as if it were some commercial product. But there's no need to be a professional sociologist to know that political regimes cannot be treated in isolation from the rest of the social structure. Society forms a whole, with interdependent elements. The effects of a new measure do not depend solely on the intrinsic qualities of this measure. If you introduce medical protection alone, without touching anything else, the result is a sudden rise in the birthrate, which in turn leads to an exodus from the countryside and social tensions. If you open the border to manufactured products, you destroy the local subsistence economy and encourage a slide from poverty to real destitution. If you plonk democratic rules onto a traditional society, you can't be sure of the result. The advantages of each regime are inseparable from its disadvantages; introducing it in a mechanical way risks encouraging the latter to the detriment of the former.

We were able to observe this in 2001 in Afghanistan and in 2003 in Iraq. The Taliban regime deserved to be condemned, but its overthrow did not lead to an American-style democracy, nor could it have done so: the other ingredients of a liberal society were lacking. In a large part of the country, power passed from the hands of the Taliban into those of local warlords; it's not certain that the daily life of the Afghans, and even of Afghani women, has been improved. In Iraq, the toppling of the dictatorship has left a power vacuum, which the victorious American army has been unable to fill. There ensued a period of pillaging and insecurity which has aggravated the situation of the population even more. There is nothing surprising in this chain of events: as every one knows, there is something worse than a bad state, namely the absence of any state. Anarchy is worse than tyranny, since it replaces the arbitrary whim of one by the arbitrary whim of all.

In addition, even supposing a democratic government is finally established, nothing guarantees that it will be liberal in inspiration, or that it will protect the liberties of all individuals. That power lies in the hands of the people in no way guarantees that it will be good: the "people" may also decide, for instance, that women should stay at home, or that the death penalty and corporal punishment should be applied without restraint. An Islamic republic may be imposed by the will of the people: in this sense it will be democratic, but it will not have contributed to the well-being of the whole population.

The example of Kosovo, which is often mentioned in this context, is not very convincing either. The aim of the intervention was to prevent ethnic cleansing (the genocide that had been announced was a propaganda measure, not a real threat): the effect of the intervention was to make ethnic cleansing a definitive reality, with all the Serbs on one side, and all the Albanians on the other, and neither of the two groups daring to venture into their neighbor's lands. The aim was to build democracy instead of tyranny; it helped to establish a territory ruled by various mafias, a crossroads for European prostitution and drugs trafficking. "In the absence of public order, in the absence of police and tribunals, Kosovo became an ideal terrain for every kind of crime," writes the Kosovar journalist Veton Surroi.[3] Unemployment in this area has hit 90 percent; the province lives mainly off European handouts. The persecution of Albanian speakers by the central Yugoslav power has ceased, and this is indisputably a good thing; but can the transformation of the province into a UN protectorate, dependent on financial aid, really be considered as a model for the settling of inter-ethnic tensions? Unless the aim of the intervention was not really altogether different, as the ex-commander of NATO, General Wesley Clark, now says: "No particular target, or set of targets, was as important as the cohesion of NATO."[4] But in that case, one cannot help asking, does the safeguard of any institution – even NATO – justify the sacrifice of human lives?

Preventive war, started not because of any real attack, but because of a *feeling* of insecurity, is based on an evaluation of the situation which is necessarily partial and subjective. The example of the United States risks becoming contagious: if we accept that every country attacks others merely on the basis of its own evaluation of the situation, the way lies open for a permanent war of all against all.

It's true that tyrannies are hateful. Many Afghanis yesterday, and many Iraqis today, both inside and outside the country, wished for foreign intervention to drive out the hated figures in power. But were they ready to accept all the consequences of their gesture? Let's imagine that, tomorrow, they become the leaders of a new government: will they accept that the destiny of their country be decided elsewhere than in their own country? Or that foreign powers may depose them when their policy no longer pleases them? In other words, are they ready to submit tomorrow to a rule which harms them – the selfsame rule which, today, turns out to their advantage?

The second objective pursued by this war was victory over terrorism and thus the reinforcement of national security. Can we say it was attained? The war in Afghanistan most certainly diminished the immediate threat of terrorist attacks; as we have seen, the link between the Iraqi regime and the Islamic networks was much more problematic. We have to say above all that traditional war – bombings, destruction, occupation – isn't the appropriate means of combating the new enemy. The United States was to some degree lucky that one country – Afghanistan – declared its solidarity with that network; a traditional military counterattack thus became possible. However, there's a risk that the Afghan way of claiming responsibility for the attacks – which once more illustrates the political ineptitude of aggressors who preferred to throw their weight around rather than to vanish into thin air – won't happen again; and this will make the fight against terrorist aggressions much more difficult. The problem here comes from the fact that the aggression is perpetrated by individuals without any definite territory. Technological progress has made it possible to put dangerous weapons into the hands of isolated characters, and not just states. These people manage to hide without too much difficulty, and thus evade any military response. As well as that, these same individuals serenely envisage the sacrifice of their own lives; the usual preventive actions thus hold no terrors for them.

The United States can these days win any confrontation of the traditional kind: so much seems clear. But, when faced with the terrorist threat, they somewhat resemble a boxer who tries to swat flies without taking off his gloves. Laser missiles and bombs should here give way to quite different methods: infiltrating networks, tailing and bugging suspects, blocking the flow of funds, abducting or executing particularly dangerous individuals, and propaganda. At the same time, terrorists must be isolated from their bases: with this aim in view, and without yielding to blackmail, it is necessary to suppress the causes of resentment, the injustices for which one is responsible and which ensure the population's visceral support for the terrorists. If an entire population considers that the terrorists' cause is just, the fight against them has little chance of succeeding: this is the bitter lesson that France learned from the war in Algeria, where its military superiority was nonetheless undeniable.

From this point of view, it is far from certain that the war in Iraq really contributed to the eradication of terrorism. Violence breeds violence: this formula, however banal, is nonetheless true. This war will inevitably be felt as a humiliation by several Arab, Muslim, or merely non-Western populations. And humiliation, real or imagined, is the mother of fanaticism; nothing feeds terrorism more effectively than the convergence between an aptitude for self-sacrifice and a technology of destruction that has become accessible to all. Since the end of the war, the attacks have resumed; terrorism is doing just fine.

The positive effects that people had hoped for from the war remain deeply problematic. Conversely, certain negative effects are undeniable. To begin with, the damage inflicted on Iraq, the country and its population. I won't try to rival the ancient and modern authors who have described the disasters of war in overwhelming terms; but a few obvious facts need to be recalled. And we must never forget that behind those abstract words – "war," "victory," "liberation" – are hidden mangled bodies and destroyed houses. Every individual is unique and irreplaceable, and the life of every single human being is priceless; to factor the number of victims one will create into one's strategic calculations is obscene. These individuals do not live alone, they are the object of the love of those close to them, whose lives will be definitively turned upside down: men and women, fathers and mothers, sons and daughters, doomed to brood until the day they die over the death of someone they cherished more than anything else in the world, and who will never return. Which pitiless god is it who decides that regime change justifies the sacrifice of 1,000, or 10,000, or 100,000 lives, and the ineffaceable suffering of ten times more human beings who were close to them? How can anyone see themselves as standing so far outside the human community (or, conversely, see the "enemy" population as standing so far outside it) as to decide, as at the time of the bombing of Hiroshima, that a quarter of a million human lives is a reasonable price to pay in order to bring about a swifter victory?

Even the separation between civil and military victims here becomes factitious: what are soldiers if not boys who were civilians just a few months earlier and who are destined to become so again a few months later? Beyond the present, there is the future: the wounded condemned to remain mutilated, sickly, lame; the children condemned to grow up without parents, doomed to a life of bitterness, revolt, and dreams of vengeance. Beyond individual human beings, there is the whole framework within which lives are led: the houses, with all that has been accumulated in them over the years, projections of one's identity outside of oneself. The streets and roads that link them together. The buildings, fields, and landscapes, transformed into ruins, wastelands, and gutted vacancy. It is this, together with so many other sufferings experienced by anonymous individuals, that we agree to consider as a negligible quantity when we choose to attain our aims rapidly by means of war rather than slowly via negotiation and the exerting of pressure.

How many deaths were caused by this war in Iraq? We know the exact number of victims on the Anglo-American side – 150 persons – but not that of the Iraqi dead. Complete figures are lacking – but we can hazard a guess. For example, it has been estimated that during the first incursion of the American tanks into the suburbs of Baghdad, which lasted a mere three hours, there will have been 2,000 to 3,000 Iraqis dead for every one American killed.[5] Several divisions of the Iraqi army were destroyed, it is said, as if they had fallen into a "meat mincer." The *Financial Times* of 11 April 2003 puts forward an estimate: around 30,000 Iraqi military personnel killed, together with an indefinite number of civilians. Such was the effect of the 24,000 bombs dropped, the 800 missiles fired, the countless rifle shots: is there anything surprising about it? Weapons are made to kill with; and kill they do. Likewise, does anyone have the right to draw any consolation from the claim that the war might have been much more murderous (this is the reason why General Jay Garner found it a "merciful" war)? Do you really become a benefactor of mankind because you haven't killed as many people as you might have done?

There is no reason at all to be proud of the effects of the war on the enemy, even if the "fall of the tyrant" was desirable. Its effects on third parties – the peoples who remained outside the conflict – are not all positive either. Of course, nobody any longer has any doubts – if they still did – about American military superiority; unless they have a death wish, nobody will defy the United States in *that* area. But the country's prestige did not increase as a result: this demonstration of brute force, this choice not to heed the objections and reservations, provoked a general feeling of hostility. Feelings, admittedly, are not directly convertible into armored divisions; but they may, one day, encourage violent reactions. I'm not only talking about the populations of the Third World, who are now brooding over their resentments, but also about the United States' traditional allies, such as the Western European countries in which the image of America has been damaged. It was with perplexity and some disquiet that I read the results of a poll (28–29 March 2003) which found that while the conflict was still raging, only a third of the French felt more on the Anglo-American side, while a quarter were opting for an Iraqi victory! A gut reaction, no doubt, but a revealing one all the same: unlike the military forces, those who promoted the war on the international image market lost their wager.

Finally, negative effects have made themselves felt in public life within the United States. War conditions did not fail to dent certain principles of democracy (this is one of the permanent dangers of war). The most obvious infraction of the liberal and democratic spirit concerns the treatment of prisoners of war in Afghanistan – a treatment rendered possible by the current war atmosphere. In order to bypass the legal obligations that force it to grant certain rights to prisoners, the United States government kept them outside its territory, in Afghanistan itself or on the military base at Guantánamo Bay, in Cuba. In conformity with the letter of the law – but what a betrayal of its spirit! What's more, this is not a mere internment, but a form of treatment very difficult to distinguish from torture. The American officials, as reported in the *New York Times* of 12 March 2003, consider as acceptable techniques of interrogation "sleep and light deprivation and the temporary withholding of food, water, access to sunlight and medical attention."[6] The usual "pressurizing" techniques include "covering suspects' heads with black hoods for hours at a time and forcing them to stand or kneel in uncomfortable positions in extreme cold or heat," from over 40 degrees to minus 10.[7] Certain prisoners are forced to remain naked for long hours, their hands and feet bound. If this isn't physical torture, it's something remarkably similar. The relative inefficiency of these methods – always justified by the need to extract confessions as a matter of urgency so as to prevent future attacks – could have been learnt by the American military from their French counterparts, who resorted systematically to torture during the Algerian War, with the eventual result that everyone knows. But it seems that we never learn from others' mistakes.

Although less flagrant, other infractions of the forms of life characteristic of a liberal democracy were just as regrettable. By virtue of an emergency law, the Patriot Act, certain groups in the American population (people of Iraqi origin, Arabs, Muslims) were subjected to various kinds of discrimination, and public liberties were suspended, leading to detention beyond the authorized limits, telephone tapping, and various threats.

Over and above these measures adopted by the American government, the war situation creates a certain atmosphere that is hardly favorable to the affirmation of democratic values. The most obvious, for a visitor from abroad, throughout the conflict, was the drastic reduction in the pluralism of information – the effect, not of censorship imposed by the government, but rather of self-censorship, justified by the need to show support for the troops. The more the spectator watched or listened to certain television channels, the more he gained the impression that they were the ones who were deciding the outcome of the war – so much did information take second place to propaganda. In Europe, admittedly, the situation was highly unusual: public opinion in these countries was generally hostile to the war, but the United States was nonetheless the traditional ally; as a result, divergent viewpoints found themselves cheek by jowl on television screens or in the press. Conversely, the American media seemed, on the whole, always to present their information with a very broad brush, being more concerned to carry conviction than to seek the truth. Such a choice doesn't imply that you lie or falsify the facts: all it needs is for you to select the news with a very definite agenda in view. Reality is sufficiently complex to provide evidence for pretty much any thesis.

The rising intolerance towards dissident opinions was also a sign of the deterioration of democratic life. Its effects can be brutal, especially when those Western ayatollahs, the media bosses, launch a fatwa against whichever public figure has expressed his or her disapproval of the war. Is it right for artists or musicians to be boycotted and deprived of the channels of communication, for their disks to be burned or discarded, for them to be covered in defamatory insults? American society has always exercised a stronger pressure on individual behavior than Western European societies; but in time of war this pressure is notched up a few degrees, and starts to become quite alarming.

The exacerbation of patriotic passions doesn't contribute to fighting against ethnocentrism and xenophobia, attitudes that are far from democratic. American public opinion was indignant at the sight of "its" captured and imprisoned soldiers being paraded on Iraqi television; it had no problem with seeing Iraqi soldiers who had been imprisoned, since the latter had no right to the respect due to the dignity of individuals. Nor was it disturbed at discovering that some 50 Iraqi leaders had been reduced to the status of playing cards, and that the order had been issued to take them "dead or alive" – in other words, to liquidate them, if necessary, without further ado. The proliferation of euphemisms is a bad sign, too. To say that "a division has suffered significant losses" is more polite, but no less grave, than to announce the death of 1,000 or 2,000 men.

Finally, another deterioration has become apparent, more difficult to grasp but also more dangerous for the democratic way of life. It consists in making unacceptable practices acceptable, as if the urgency of the situation was sufficient to justify anything and everything. Take, for example, the proofs of the guilt of Iraq. The nuclear threat that the country was alleged to represent was backed up by two documents that were both revealed to be false: a contract with Niger and a supposedly secret report which was in reality a student's thesis. Were the American authorities really unaware of this, or did they in turn prefer victory to truth? Observing the leadership of the country, it was difficult not to think of the means formerly used by the enemies of democracy: demagogy, the manipulation of public opinion, the lack of transparency in decision making. The recent history of the United States shows that this threat is not necessarily imaginary: it was, after all, there that McCarthyism flourished, that dangerous perversion of the liberal order. We can't avoid asking whether the reinforcement of democracy in Iraq really justifies its undermining in the United States.

– 4 –

In Praise of Pluralism

The national interest of the United States is not well served by the policies exemplified by the war in Iraq. As Raymond Aron wisely noted, "having great power is not the only way of being great"[1] – no more, one might add, than military success is the only form of success. In the medium and long term, this policy leads to a degradation of democratic life *within* the United States; it tarnishes the image of the US in the eyes of other countries by nourishing an anti-Americanism that may become dangerous; the benefit constituted by the toppling of the dictatorship is in turn counterbalanced by the inevitable damage brought about by every war and by the political uncertainties that ensue. This deployment of brute force, without any attention to the judgments to which it gives rise, is in reality quite dangerous: ideas and feelings, though apparently impotent, can overthrow empires. Whilst even within the country this policy leads to depriving peaceful projects of the support it gives the military, and thereby impoverishes the country, it produces a climate of instability and risk in other countries. The security of the country is better served by respect for national sovereignty than by preventive war.

It is of course possible to admit that war is the continuation of politics by other means, since it is always a question of defending the national interest. But the opposite is by no means true: politics is not war in disguise. The "other means" even spell out the end of politics: war is an admission of failure, the sign that, now that all political means have been exhausted, nothing is left but to resort to brute force. When weapons speak, words fall silent; but politics is essentially a matter of words and negotiations, the quest for compromise and consensus.

Military power can constrain bodies, but its effects on hearts and minds are much more problematic; and winning over hearts and minds is no less necessary for the security of the United States than is victory in war. This is particularly true as far as the terrorist threat is concerned, since it is not embodied in the form of a regular army. From this point of view the French Minister for Foreign Affairs, Dominique de Villepin, was right when he told the UN Security Council on 19 March 2003: "In a world where the threat is asymmetrical, where the weak defy the strong, the power of conviction, the ability to sway opinion count as much as the number of military divisions."[2]

United States interests would be better preserved if it renounced this risky policy which might lead to its using, tomorrow, first-strike nuclear weapons, and if, instead of this policy, it took pains to legitimate its actions in the eyes of the rest of the world. But what enables a policy to be legitimated? Many thinkers in the past have debated this question at length, and pondered on the principles of political right. It is not the mere fact of holding power, since this is often originally acquired by violence (the War of Independence presides over American democracy, just as does the 1789 Revolution over French democracy). And even when power is the legal expression of the popular will, it can get things wrong: majority opinion is not necessarily enlightened, and may also act against the spirit of justice. Nor does legitimacy come from the noble aims that we claim to be pursuing: the powerful will always be suspected of using them to dissimulate its selfish desires. So where *can* legitimacy be found?

It was Montesquieu, in the eighteenth century, who came up with the answer in this brief formula: "unlimited authority can never be legitimate."[3] It is neither the origin which legitimates, nor the aim; it is the very way in which power is exercised. And this involves imposing limits on it, and hence sharing it with others. Two different conceptions here find themselves locked in conflict: one which appeals to unity and one which appeals to plurality. The former believes it possesses the Good, and in consequence considers itself to have the right to impose it on everyone. The latter also hopes that it has the best way of looking at things, but it doesn't allow itself to count on it, and thinks that the sharing out and separation of powers is preferable to their unification. Several political parties are better than one, even if the latter is the best of them. Within a country, the limitation of power comes from the mutual independence of executive, legislative, and judiciary, as well as from the plurality of political parties and sources of information, or indeed from the granting of rights to minorities. In international life, it comes from respect for the sovereignty of other states, even if one is powerful enough to subdue them, and from respect for the treaties and conventions between countries, even if one is in a position to transgress them. This acceptance of pluralism is the best means of protecting the autonomy of each, and thereby obtaining its agreement.

Treaties between countries or obligations towards an international organization such as the United Nations do not have the same binding force of the laws that govern life within a country; but as they are a voluntarily accepted restriction of the use of force, they are part and parcel of the pluralist division of world power. But at the moment it went to war against Iraq, the United States treated these international conventions with a certain amount of disdain. It has to be said that their intentions had been clearly formulated in *The National Security Strategy*. Here, you could read the following words: "While the United States will constantly strive to enlist the support of the international community, we will not hesitate to act alone, if necessary, to exercise our right of self-defense by acting pre-emptively against such terrorists."[4] In other words, the legitimacy granted by the UN is a camouflage – desirable but not necessary – for force. The negative effect of such declarations is difficult to measure.

It is often said, as against the pluralist ideal in international relations, that you appeal to right, to the rules, to the respect owed to the weak, only when you yourself are weak; if only you were strong, you would cheerfully transgress these conventions to satisfy your desires without further ado. This argument goes back a long way: one character, in Plato's *Republic*, refers to the legend of Gyges, who possesses a ring which can make him invisible, and thereby ensure he has absolute power. Thus he can steal, become wealthy, kill, and seize power. How many people would have the necessary firmness of soul to resist temptation, if Gyges' ring were theirs? How many would renounce the omnipotence that would bring them close to the level of the gods? If we can believe the legend, "no man is just of his own free will, but only under compulsion."[5] But this conception of man is wrong in two respects: first, because the principles of justice are not matters of pure convention and their transgression brings inner suffering to the transgressor himself; but above all because the proper exercise of power, which involves sharing it, serves the best interests of the one who wields power in the right way, in that it ensures he wins the benevolence of the others and their support for a common endeavor.

It is also often claimed that pluralism is not something you decree, but something you discover to be already present in the situation; but the United States is already, on the military level, much stronger than any other power on earth – stronger even than all of them put together. Are we supposed to wish for a new arms race, so as to restore the balance of power? Of course not. The fact that the United States possesses the greatest military force in the world is one thing; that it can use it to obtain the immediate satisfaction of its desires is another. We are not talking about another constraint, this time imposed on the American government, but about a voluntary self-limitation in the exercise of power, in the name of the interests of the country as properly understood.

People also sometimes wonder whether a pluralist world (a "multipolar" world as it is called these days) would not be condemned to permanent confrontation, with each member trying at every moment to outdo the others. Doesn't the initial equality encourage competition? Isn't the peace of empire, the definitive submission to the greatest power, preferable for the tranquility of all? But we're not obliged to choose between these brutal alternatives, war or submission. When it comes to international relations, the adage (an echo of one which comes from the Gospels, alas) "he who is not with us is against us" is not applicable. The simplistic schema "friend/enemy" may be very widespread, but it doesn't explain the diversity of relations between different countries. These relations can extend from active partnership to peaceful competition, via sporadic collaboration or neutrality. This international equilibrium will not be definitive – but surely this flexibility, this ability to meet the unexpected, is preferable to an order that is fixed once and for all? Here I concur with Kant's (far from angelic) conclusion: he said he preferred the coexistence of states to their union under a "universal monarch," and the balance of power established between them, despite the struggle resulting from their diversity, to the definitive peace imposed by empire.[6]

A power such as the United States will obviously never renounce the use of force. But this doesn't mean that it can abandon itself to the intoxication of knowing that it's the strongest, together with the rousing conviction that it is the most just. Pride is rarely a wise counselor. It is in the interests of the United States to accept voluntary limitations to the use of its power, as indeed certain voices – far from anti-American – within the country itself recommend. In this case, military force should be used only in legitimate defense, in the case of aggression against oneself (as in Afghanistan) or against one's allies (as in Kuwait). The rest of the time, one should, as far as military action goes, respect the international order, however imperfect it may be, and national sovereignty, however hateful may be the regimes that shelter behind it; but one should try to transform these regimes by peaceful means – which themselves, it should be remembered, are not lacking in power.

— 5 —

Might or Right?

The American strategy in the conflict with Iraq was criticized in numerous countries, including certain Allied governments, foremost amongst which was France. The most
frequently used argument was that the United States was
conducting a policy of force, whereas international relations ought to obey right, as embodied in this case by the
United Nations, its Security Council, and their resolutions.
On 7 March 2003, just a few days before the outbreak of
hostilities, Dominique de Villepin announced to the Security Council, "There may be some who believe that these
problems can be resolved by force, thereby creating a new
order. This is not France's conviction."[1] On 18 March
2003, on the eve of the invasion, President Chirac decided
to justify his position to the Security Council by declaring
to the press that, unlike the United States, which sought to
"prefer the use of force to compliance with the law," France
"has acted in the name of the primacy of the law and in
accordance with her conception of relations between
peoples and between nations."[2] He thus asked that steps
be taken to "ensure the respect of international legality."[3]

Once war had commenced, the French leaders did not
change their minds. Speaking to the International Institute

of Strategic Affairs in London on 27 March 2003, Villepin reiterated his faith in the "collective norms [. . .] defined to contain the use of force," adding, "only consensus and respect for law can give force the legitimacy it needs."[4] He concluded, "Force must serve the law." He returned to this theme, once the war was over, in an interview: "The role of the UN is more than ever irreplaceable," he declared. "The United Nations embody a universal conscience over and above individual states": the UN constitutes a step towards the "constitution of a world democracy."[5] Other European leaders also expressed the opinion that today the reign of force is coming to an end, and that it is progressively being replaced by the rule of law; as a result, war could be definitively banished.

Such a vision of the world is obviously enticing. But before we accept it, we need to ask ourselves, does it account for the world as it really exists? Or might we be in the process of taking our desires for realities? In order to judge a situation correctly, we need to know it; but we won't find the truth if we know in advance that it must be in conformity with the Good. Is the reign of right over might a reality, or are we dealing with an illusion, one which seems flattering now, but one which risks leading our decisions astray? Are "international legality" and "world democracy" anything other than juridical functions?

During the eighteenth-century Enlightenment, contributors to the French *Encyclopédie*, and other philosophers and intellectuals, nursed the hope that the progress of civilization within each country would spread to relations between countries; the whole world could then be thought of as a "general society" of which the individual societies would be, as it were, the citizens. It was Jean-Jacques Rousseau who took on the task of sweeping away their fragile constructions. "Between one man and another," he wrote, "we live in a civil state, subject to laws; between one people and another, each one enjoys natural freedom."[6] In other words, between countries, relations remain in the state of nature; in each individual country, however, reigns the state of society. Why should this be the case? Because the citizens of every country have renounced the use of violence, handing it over to the state which includes them all; individual countries, however, do not form part of a universal state, and do not recognize any authority to which they could delegate their force; so they keep it for themselves. Unless they are threatened by a common enemy – which might come from another planet, for instance – states elevate the particular interest over the general interest (as is illustrated by, among other things, the difficulties encountered in the quest for agreement over subjects such as global warming).

All states experience this dual structure: the same principles do not govern policy at home and abroad. At home, might is subject to right, the army takes orders from the government, and the police ensures the functioning of justice. Abroad, it is might which governs relations between countries, tempered solely by the contracts they establish between themselves voluntarily, but which they can also break at any moment. International law does not have the same effectiveness as national law, since it does not possess – as national law does – an armed wing (unless states voluntarily accept this law). Rather than being subject to law, relations between countries depend on an international *order*, comprised of treaties, conventions, and participation in international organizations; but this order is not guaranteed by a world police – which does not exist, any more than does a universal state. This is why it is somewhat pointless to speak, as some people did during the conflict with Iraq, of an "illegal war." By definition, war – all war – breaks down the pre-existing international order; but the latter was never endowed with force of law.

So it is futile to refer in this context to the "supremacy of law," "respect for law," or "collective norms": the contracts that exist between countries, contracts that it has always been permissible to break unilaterally, are not laws;

what is called "international law" simply does not belong to the same category as military power. It is true that this line of reasoning doesn't apply to countries that belong to the European Union in their mutual relations: the latter have renounced the use, between themselves, of armed force. But this renunciation does not extend beyond the frontiers of the Union: wars with countries outside it are conceivable, and no law can forbid them.

So where does this leave the role of the UN, an organization that includes all the countries in the world? Isn't the UN an embodiment of the way that might can be curbed by right? In order to abandon this illusion, we need to remember that at the basis of the UN lies a choice that is not founded in any right – namely, the granting of the "right of veto" to the five permanent members of the Security Council. In other words, those five members – the great powers – are exempt from the obligations weighing on the others, since they can impose their veto on any resolution that concerns them. A great power can do no wrong! Thus the USSR, quite recently, escaped any condemnation that might have led to intervention, since it could prevent any resolution concerning its acts. This protection can be extended, from the "veto members" to their allies: in this way Israel, protected by the United States, doesn't risk having to face any intervention decided by the United Nations. So, far from restricting the hegemony of the great powers, the world organization sanctions it.

It must be added that, even when the UN was not paralyzed by one of these great powers, it hardly showed itself as a stirring embodiment of justice on the march. There have been numerous massacres that the UN was unable or unwilling to prevent: genocide in Cambodia and Rwanda, civil war in Angola and Sierra Leone . . . The reasons in each case are different, but they spring from a common origin: the ineffectual nature of an organization which does not have its own armed force, but has to call on that of each individual country – to which we can add the inevitable ponderousness of a distant bureaucratic machine, and the divergences of interests of the member states, always ready as they are to put a spoke in its wheel.

It is far from being the case that the conduct of all states is dictated by mere considerations of right. It's worth recalling how, in March 2003, yet again in relation to Iraq, the American and French envoys jetted round the world, seeking to exert pressure or promise rewards, with the view of obtaining a vote in favor from this or that country. Can we really see this as a manifestation of that "universal conscience" mentioned by de Villepin? Can we see it as a triumph of justice in the functioning of the UN Commission of Human Rights (currently presided over by Libya!), which has never sought to condemn for their infractions of human rights countries such as China or Vietnam, Algeria or Syria, Sudan or Zimbabwe?

During the Iraq crisis, the UN had a real problem on its hands. Its Security Council had to choose between two unpleasant solutions: either submit to the United States, and thereby show its servility, or oppose the US, and thereby show its impotence. It opted for the second, and it might be claimed in its defense that it thereby saved its honor; its weakness was nonetheless openly revealed. The Lilliputians who tried to shackle Gulliver with numberless chains all scattered and fled as soon as the giant decided to rise to his feet. France was crowing about having won the battle at the UN – but it lost the battle that was being fought outside the council chambers, since the war really did take place. Now a policy is judged, not by its intentions, but by its results; so it was a bad policy.

In addition, France itself, very ticklish on questions of right when these questions concern stronger countries, doesn't always submit to the UN when its own affairs are at stake. General de Gaulle did not miss a single opportunity of declaring in advance his refusal to kowtow to an organization in which so many dictators had a seat. Even in 2003, France did not altogether renounce the temptation of "resolving these problems by force," in de Villepin's

words. It did not ask for UN authorization to intervene in
the Ivory Coast, and doubtless this was a good thing: new
massacres would probably have taken place before the
necessary consensus could have been obtained. One can't
help thinking that if, during the Iraq crisis, France insisted
so much on the necessity of going through the UN and its
Security Council, it was because this was the only place
where it could assume the role of a world power.

The same could be said of the hopes placed in international justice as a means of imposing right throughout the world: the effect of all this was the creation
of an International Criminal Tribunal to judge Yugoslav
or Rwandan nationals, or else the plan for an International Criminal Court, designed to function in permanent
sitting. The good intentions behind these initiatives are
undeniable; their consequences are not always so. For in
this situation, one of two things must follow.

On the one hand you sacrifice effectiveness to equity. But
in this case the justice for which you are fighting stops at
the door of the great powers – which, in our world, are
not only the United States but also Russia, China, India,
and a few others. Raymond Aron put it like this: "A great
power accepts no order and will not be constrained."[7] The
process whereby the International Criminal Court was
established speaks volumes. Several countries voted against
its creation: the United States, India, China, Vietnam,
Israel, Bahrain, and Qatar. We may well think that even if
Russia voted for it, this doesn't prove that it would submit
to the Court's injunctions. The new American President
declared, on his election, that he would never ratify the
convention legalizing the Court. But even if he had signed
the agreement, the result would still have been problematic: the United States never bows to the demands made of
it by the different international commissions, even those
created by the UN, when those demands concern its activ-
ities in Latin America – or, more simply, its interests.

On the other hand you sacrifice equity to effectiveness. In this case, you place at the service of justice a powerful army – that of NATO, or that of the United States – but at the risk of seeing this army serving its own interests rather than those of justice. Louise Arbour, former prosecutor for the ICC, remarked with a certain ingenuousness, "Only with difficulty can the military renounce the whole spectrum of nation-states to perceive their operations."[8] This didn't stop her appealing to the same military, and even placing herself at their service, by giving juridical endorsement to NATO's action in Yugoslavia. How could it then be possible to maintain one's impartiality? Everyone knows how the accusation of war crimes committed by NATO was treated: the tribunal contented itself with entrusting the inquiry into its own possible partiality to its own functionaries – who, quite unsurprisingly, came up with a whitewash, declaring themselves to be above all suspicion. This wasn't the opinion of certain NGOs, or of the International Committee of the Red Cross, which could hardly be suspected of harboring sympathies for Milošević and declared in its report on this question, "Such a difference in approach, depending on whether the alleged war crimes are imputed to Yugoslavia or NATO, is really shocking."[9]

Is selective justice, which strikes only one's enemies, still justice? This question could be asked not only by comparing the different treatment meted out to Yugoslavia and NATO at the time of the Balkan conflict, but elsewhere, too. Take, for example, the policy towards minorities: that of Yugoslavia could indeed be criticized, but couldn't the same be said of the policy practiced in Israel or Turkey? Those countries do not accept international intervention any more than Yugoslavia, even leaving aside the question of justice; and yet they have never been punished. Why not? The reason is that they are "friendly" countries, countries that are strategically useful to "us." This is a reality that, of course, shouldn't be ignored – but it no longer has anything to do with justice.

The dream of a universal justice that would supplant the justice of individual nations brings a whole host of problems in its train. For while any judiciary decision is universal, the community which has to take the consequences of it is merely national. Imagine that a government has declared an amnesty with regard to a past civil war, while international justice decides that the statute of limitations does not apply to crimes that were committed at that time, and so they must be judged. Should international justice be obeyed, at the risk of fanning a new civil war – from which only the population of the country in question will suffer, and not the international judges? Isn't it for Chile to decide whether to judge Pinochet? Or for Cambodia to decide whether to put on trial the accomplices of Pol Pot? After all, if it isn't in the name of the people, in the name of whom or what is justice to be exercised?

Today, rather than establishing a tribunal to condemn Milošević, Pinochet, or Saddam Hussein, I wonder whether it wouldn't be more honest just to send them straightaway into exile on Saint Helena . . . Isn't the essential thing to render them incapable of causing harm? Judging the dictator after he has lost power inevitably comes down to putting him on political trial with the aim of purging and rectifying the past, transforming his strategic error into a legal crime. The fallen dictator isn't just vanquished, he is guilty as well. In order to avoid transforming the exercise of justice into a political settling of accounts, it's better to stick to the existing laws and not resort to religious or moral principles that may be absent from the legal code.

All these reflections on the deficiencies of international institutions shouldn't incite us to sabotage them even more (a contract is always preferable to chaos or blackmail); but they *should* moderate our enthusiasm. The UN can be useful in all sorts of situations; it is just that, when it comes to war, it will always be subject to the will of hegemonic states. International justice can reinforce the rule of law, especially if that justice really does govern relations between nations rather than delude itself with universal illusions. But, humanity being what it is, the international order cannot replace the will of states, and thus military power. The United Nations will never be sufficient to prevent aggression, ensure peace, and impose justice; for that, force is necessary, and force belongs to individual states. So it is pointless to contrast might and right: without might, as Pascal already realized, the melancholy truth is that right is powerless.

How can we ensure peace throughout the world? Certain countries (such as France) reply: by putting our trust in international law and organizations such as the UN. Unfortunately, this solution doesn't work: everyone knows full well that international relations do not obey the law, unless countries voluntarily decide to submit to it. Others (such as the United States) reply: by putting our trust in our strength, the greatest in the world. All other countries merely have to submit and follow this policy, even if they don't like it: that's the price you have to pay for reaping the advantage of peace. Are we condemned to this alternative? No. "Peace through law" and "peace through empire" do not exhaust the possibilities. These two replies are similar in that they seek safety in unity: the perfectly real unity of the American empire for some of them, the dreamt-of unity of world government for others. To these two options we need to add that of plurality, which contributes to the preservation of peace by the balance among several powers. It is within this framework that the Europe of tomorrow might find its place.

− 6 −

A Tranquil Power

In the contemporary world, no European country has sufficient strength to ensure, by itself, its defense against a great power; and even less to have much impact on the way the world goes. France has just learnt this lesson; during the Iraqi conflict, it defended a position which roused sympathy here and there, but had no chance of being adopted. Its military means were not up to its political ambitions. Today, each European country possesses an army that remains under national control: a force that is real but inadequate if we place ourselves within a world context.

And, on its side, the European Union doesn't have any common defense policy, nor any army at its disposal. The reasons for this situation are well known: following the Second World War, the military danger to Europe came from the USSR; however, European countries were not strong enough to defend themselves against such an adversary. So it was necessary to create the Atlantic Alliance, with NATO as a military force − one that was shared between the Europeans and the Americans, but dominated by the latter. Over the next few decades, Europeans thus benefited from the American shield, without having to assume responsibility for it. The situation was transformed only in 1989–91, with the fall of the Berlin Wall and the breakup of the USSR: since the enemy they were supposed to be defending themselves against was no longer there, the common defense policy needed rethinking – but it never happened. NATO still exists, but nobody knows what it's for anymore; and in any case, it isn't led by Europe.

In addition, even if, on various occasions, the populations of different countries seemed to be in agreement, the same is not true of governmental policies: these remain in the service of national interests. So, faced with the determination of the United States to wage war in Iraq, European countries were divided. It wasn't the first time that this absence of a European military policy made itself felt. In 1995, the European Union allowed a civil war to break out in Yugoslavia, with – among other things – massacres being committed in Bosnia: despite public indignation, no intervention was envisaged (perhaps because of conflicts of interest between France and Germany). In 1999, in a context that was admittedly more problematic, the European Union remained passive when faced with the troubles in Kosovo; military intervention did take place, but it was carried out, for the most part, by the American army. And so, once more, Europe exhibited its dependence in the military sphere.

Public opinion in numerous European countries condemned the American intervention. But it did not seek to reconcile this condemnation with the fact that Europe still depends on American military power for its security. There were two possible consistent attitudes available: either admit your military dependence and thus renounce any criticism of a policy over which you have no control (this was the option taken by the Spanish, Italian, and British governments, who had to confront their own public opinion on this issue); or protest loud and long, but then renounce the military protection offered by the United States. Trying to have it both ways was illogical. As the sociologist

Bruno Latour remarked, this meant you were condemned to a "merely moral" posture, which no longer has any "reality principle other than that of virtue, since you have shrugged off onto others the need to draw up the lines of force."[1]

If the European states do not want to be condemned to impotent hand wringing, they can choose between several solutions. Either (and this is the current position of certain countries) they can entrust their defense to a more powerful country (the United States) and rest content with approving everything their protector does. It's probably Polish President Alexander Kwasniewski who expressed this position most openly during the negotiations preceding the intervention in Iraq. Poland had just joined NATO, and he declared, "If it's President Bush's vision, it is mine."[2]

This choice of unconditional submission was followed by the "letter of the eight" European leaders, including those of Poland, Hungary, and the Czech Republic, followed in its turn by a "declaration of the ten" governments of Eastern Europe, from Estonia to Albania. As is well known, ten days later, French President Jacques Chirac scolded them in public, saying that they had "lost a fine opportunity for keeping quiet" and had behaved like "not very well brought-up children," thus even compromising their future membership of the European Union. Was this the only lesson to be learnt from this incident that occurred during the buildup to the war on Iraq?

None of the leaders of the ten countries in question has actually favored with me with their confidences. Nonetheless, it seems to me that their gesture can't be explained by a lack of upbringing, nor by an excessive gratitude towards the Americans for their role in the cold war, nor, finally, by the pressure exerted – quite overtly – by Washington.

If the countries of Eastern Europe made a point of declaring their unconditional support for United States policy, even at the risk of offending certain members of the

Union, the reason is that, to the east of their territories, there stretches another vast country: Russia. Even if the present Russian government is not involved in a policy of expansion, the quantitative disproportion between this country and the countries of Eastern Europe is such that the latter will always feel threatened by their gigantic neighbor. Those countries know what Russian domination feels like – they experienced it at first hand at the time of the Soviet Union, and in certain cases (Poland) they had experienced it for much longer. The question they cannot fail to ask is: in the case of a direct threat, will we be better protected by the United States or by the united forces of France and Germany? The answer is not in the slightest doubt. The American military shield is credible; that of France is not. Finding itself unable to match the great powers by itself, Poland prefers to be the satellite of the United States rather than of Russia: the US is a protector both more liberal and more distant.

A second solution consists in renouncing American protection without bothering to find a replacement. This is the attitude of neutral countries such as Switzerland or Austria; the pacifist temptation is well known to be just as strong in Germany. It so happened that I was crossing Germany by car, in early April 2003; I often saw posters stuck in windows: *Nie wieder Krieg!* Who wouldn't want this wish to come true? But is it enough, to achieve this, for you just to disarm yourself?

Will it be possible, one day, to "ban war"? It is doubtful. Pacifism rests sometimes on a false idea: namely, that human aggression is fading away and that violence is progressively disappearing from this world; and sometimes on a cowardly idea: namely, that no Good, and no ideal, are worth sacrificing oneself for. Negotiation is, of course, always preferable to war; unfortunately it isn't always possible. The policy of peaceful "containment" worked well against Stalin; it failed against Hitler. Today's Europeans ought to be well aware of the fact: after all, the

European Union became possible only through a military victory, that of the Allies over Nazi Germany. If the use of weapons had been voluntarily renounced, the heirs of Hitler would still be ruling over Europe.

Disarmament has never ensured peace: certain aggressors only understand the language of force. Disarmed states would be easy prey for those who have not renounced the use of weapons. And why would they hold back from conquering a Europe that is wealthy and defenceless? The politicians who would advocate this decision would jeopardize the destiny of their people. Europe as a whole cannot remain content with the path taken by Switzerland, rich and neutral: this country is protected by its exceptional position, and this wouldn't be true for the whole continent.

There remains a third solution, which consists in transforming the European Union into a military power and thus becoming in its turn an integral and active part of that pluralist order that would ensure a global balance of power – a solution that has already been proposed by several politicians, but one which until now has only been partially realized. Pluralism is preferable to unity; but for the time being, pluralism does not exist. However, this option does have one argument in its favor, and an obvious one at that: no aggression against a European country can come from within Europe. The only aggressions conceivable will originate from outside. Now in this case, what will need to be defended is the Union as a whole – and this defense will be all the more effective the more united the individual forces of the different countries turn out to be. Another obvious fact: if Europe wishes to have an autonomous policy, and free itself from the, at times, burdensome protection of the United States, it must be able to ensure its own defense by itself. If it wishes to guarantee the security of all its constituent states, those of the East as well as those of the West, it must provide itself with a significant armed force. If a European power is constituted in this way, each of the member states of the Union will lose part of its national sovereignty, but will gain in recompense a higher level of security and a far superior collective sovereignty. Only this solution, a credible response to the problems of war and peace in the world, could turn the United States away from the imperial temptation to which it is at present succumbing.

Does becoming a military power mean imitating the example of the United States, or even trying to rival it? Not necessarily. The unification of the European states within a confederation is already an unprecedented move. The form of the power to which the Union will aspire may well in turn be entirely new: we are not condemned to the choice between imperialism and impotence. I will call this form "tranquil power."

What are the tasks of this new-style military force? The European army would need to be able to do several things:

- defend the European territory against all aggression (such as that of Hitler, or that of bin Laden), if need be destroying the enemy;
- prevent all armed confrontation within the European territory itself (as in the conflicts in the former Yugoslavia or in Cyprus);
- contain by the threat of retaliation any attack by another great power (such as Russia in the time of Stalin or Brezhnev);
- intervene in the rest of the world with a rapid-reaction military force at the request of friendly governments, or prevent genocide (an intervention that will need to be more effective than those decided by the UN);
- if a privileged partner of the Union, for example the United States, is attacked, go to its aid in the name of solidarity.

At the same time, "tranquil force" implies a renunciation of other claims characteristic of imperial power. Namely:

- the European Union will not have any ambition to govern the affairs of the whole world, it will be a regional (continental) power, and not a world power; comparable to Russia and China, not to the United States. It will not seek to prevent by force an invasion of Taiwan by China, or of South Korea by North Korea, or of Kuwait by Iraq, or of India by Pakistan. This doesn't mean that it will remain indifferent to such actions, but that it will content itself with acting by other than military means. Likewise, it will not try to topple governments that it doesn't like by invading their countries, as in the case of Cuba, or Zimbabwe, or Iran – but it will seek to influence their policies. The people we dislike shouldn't be confused with the people who attack us;
- as a consequence, it will not aspire to equalling American hyperpower; the possibility of a military conflict with the United States will not be part of its strategy. It also follows that its military budget will not need to try and keep up with the American budget.

Why should Europe voluntarily renounce trying to play the part of an imperial hyperpower? Partly for reasons that stem from the past: the countries of Western Europe – Germany, Italy, France, Great Britain, Belgium, and earlier on the Netherlands, Portugal, and Spain – were indeed tempted by this role; not only do they no longer have the means, but they no longer aspire to such a position. These days they reckon that the disadvantages of such a policy far outweigh its advantages. In addition, they think that the financial means at their disposal will be more usefully spent on other programs. Finally, they consider that by renouncing preventive wars that aim to change governments that don't suit them, they are making the world a more safe and stable place. In other words, they have opted for this policy, not because it is more moral, but because it is in their interests as properly understood.

"Tranquil power" is not, for all that, a renunciation of the use of force. These days we hear mocking remarks

being addressed to "old Europe" which, so they say, has
chosen the path of Venus rather than that of Mars, and is
behaving like some sophisticated but flabby person – one
who, in a word, is lacking in virility. These are all jibes
that could already be found in the writings of the Fascist
authors who scoffed at democracy in the years following
the First World War. But Europeans refuse to have to
choose between macho characters strutting around, on the
one hand, and allegedly effeminate values, on the other;
they want to go beyond these false alternatives and provide themselves with the means to defend the way of life
they have chosen. Nor is it a question for them of choos-
ing "idealism" over "realism": no good policy can allow
itself to renounce either of them. Just as it gave the example of a peaceful unification of several states, Europe
will also be able to open the way to a calm use of power,
whose benefits are far from negligible.

As one great power among others, Europe will have, in
the current state of affairs, a privileged military partner –
the United States. The reasons for this privilege are many
and various: a long history in common, political values
(such as liberal democracy) that are generally shared, and,
finally, enemies in common. This partnership would mean
that all aggression against one party would entail the military intervention of the other, in whatever form was suitable. At the same time, if the United States were resolutely
to embark on the adventurist and revolutionary path that
seems to be tempting it at present, that partnership could
conceivably be suspended, without Europe thereby finding
itself left defenceless.

The attacks of 11 September can be considered as a
declaration of war, launched by Islamic terror. The target
that was hit was the United States, but we mustn't foster
any illusions: it was the entire West, North America and
Western (and other parts of) Europe, that they were aim-
ing at ("He who is not with us is against us," as Muslim
fundamentalists proclaim these days). Today Europeans
are spared, but tomorrow they risk being hit. On this front

(which is not that of the intervention in Iraq), as well as on certain others, a wider collaboration between American and European services is desirable. All the more now that, having been left behind in the field of conventional weapons, Europeans are probably more advanced when it comes to techniques of anti-terrorist combat, which require the recruitment of collaborators, the cooperation of witnesses, and the goodwill of the populace.

Intent on mocking French military powerlessness, Gary Schmitt, director of the neo-fundamentalist group New American Century, said, "If France wants to put 30,000 men in South Korea, they only have to tell us! If they want to put an aircraft carrier in the strait of Taiwan, they only have to tell us!"[3] He thereby demonstrated that he was a whole war behind. Wars of confrontation between states are not the most difficult to win, and the means of retaliation at the disposal of a great power are of such a kind that, at all events, aggression is highly unlikely. It isn't ships or tanks, after all, that will prevent desperate and fanatical people from carrying out suicide attacks that lead to thousands of deaths. The United States doesn't need any French aircraft carriers; but they will find their intelligence services very useful.

This is what a common European defense policy might mean.

— 7 —

European Values

What would be the use of having a European armed force? To defend a certain identity that Europeans hold dear.

Any inhabitant of Europe is aware first and foremost of the diversity of the countries that make it up: each possesses its own language, customs, and problems. And yet, in the lead-up to the intervention in Iraq, it was striking to see how much public opinion, in each country, stayed similar. This kinship went beyond the contradictory positions adopted by their governments: Spanish and Italian citizens were of the same mind as the Germans and the French, and even the support of the British for the war was fragile. The crisis thus brought out a division that had already been around for quite a while; what a contrast between the disagreements of politicians and the unforced mutual understanding of the citizens! The former give the impression, when they debate European institutions, that what they are most intent on is not losing a scrap of the power they enjoy on the national level. The latter, in particular when they are young, cross frontiers without even thinking about it, move with the greatest of ease from one capital to another, and find it perfectly natural to sit down to a meal between a woman from Finland and one from

Greece, or a man from Denmark and one from Austria. The "Erasmus" programs which enable European students to pursue their studies outside their countries of origin, have over the past years encouraged the development of this European sensibility.

Seen from outside, Europe gives an even greater impression of forming a unity. Bulgaria is situated within the European continent, but, in my childhood, we talked of Europe as being a desirable territory, starting at Venice or Vienna. Of course, "Europe" meant for us first and foremost the quality of manufactured goods, in comparison with their local equivalents: the blades of "European" razors gave a closer shave, the pants imported from "Europe" were more becoming, "European" electric gadgets lasted longer. But this wasn't the only thing: over and above its material advantages, "Europe" enjoyed a prestige, a reputation for spiritual superiority that we would have found it difficult to analyze but of which we were no less convinced.

The idea of a common European mentality is nothing new. Reflecting on the conditions of a decent international life, Jean-Jacques Rousseau said that "all the powers of Europe form between themselves a sort of system," not so much through the treaties that link them than through "the union of interests, the interrelation of their moral guidelines, and the conformity of their customs."[1] In Rousseau's time, this "system" existed in people's minds, but it was contradicted by the facts: conflicts between European countries were common.

Rousseau already knew from whence sprang this closeness of outlook: it stems from a common history and geography. European countries are all heirs of a civilization that established itself on the continent more than 25 centuries ago, in Greece and later in Rome. They have all been marked by the Christian religion, which has continually asserted itself and maintained its contradictory relations with Judaism and Islam. They benefited from a shared, rapid technological development, from the Renaissance

onwards, and certain of them embarked, from the six-
teenth century onwards, on colonial conquests to the four
corners of the world – before seeing, a few centuries later,
the former colonized coming to live among them in the
old metropolises. These diverse ingredients from their past,
together with many others, are things that Europeans neither can nor will forget: they live in the middle of a land-
scape that is profoundly transformed by human labor, in
cities whose creation goes back thousands of years, amid
monuments and remains that form a part of their identity.
For this reason, it is perfectly legitimate to describe Europe
– so long as we mean *all* of Europe – as "old."

European countries have often waged war on one another. Their peoples are not ready to forget the hecatomb
of the First World War: the smallest French village has its
monument to the dead, with its long list of victims; even
today, children still get injured playing with unexploded
bombs. In the twentieth century, European countries suffered under totalitarian oppression: first the Communist
dictatorship, in the East, and then the Nazi terror, in the
West, before becoming the scene of a generalized confrontation in the Second World War, accompanied by countless crimes and by the Nazi extermination of "inferior
races," Jews, and Gypsies. The Communist system emerged
strengthened from all this, and spread even further, before
being contained in the course of the cold war. All these
events constitute the painful heritage of "old Europe." If
Europe has, these days, renounced its imperial ambitions,
it's because it knows all too well the costs.

As for geography, it's the very cramming together of so
many peoples in the limited space of Europe that constitutes its most striking characteristic. It's impossible to travel
two hours in a plane, these days, without finding oneself
in a different country: a foreign language, an exotic way
of life. This prominent cape of the continent of Asia is
hardly bigger in surface area than the United States or
China; but on its territory you can find some 40 or so
autonomous states instead of just one.

But contemporary European identity is not a mere historical or geographical given, even if it derives from it. Taken out of their original context, certain values have come together in what might be called the European project – and participation in this project is open to all people of good will, wherever they come from. Their source is local, but their appeal is universal.

So the European continent possesses one striking characteristic: war between the countries that constitute it became, just a short while ago, inconceivable. This fact, unique in the history of the world, is astonishing and needs to be reflected on: what is the mentality that made it possible? What are the "moral guidelines," as Rousseau put it, that finally dictated what actions were taken?

People are often hesitant to enumerate the political values of Europe: even if we leave aside the spiritual and cultural values that do not entail any direct political consequences, there is a fear that we may be reproached for a certain naivety or a degree of complacency. Europeans have no desire to produce an over-pretentious image of themselves, one that doesn't correspond to the reality. On the other hand, European values are obviously to be found outside Europe, either because they belong to all men and women, or because European ideas have been spread abroad. However, on closer examination, they are not found there to the same degree, nor do they form the same patterns. And today, when European construction is entering on a decisive phase, it may be useful to take the risk of seeming naive and naming those values, even if only to start an open debate. It isn't my aim to draw up a list of contrasts or to point out what other cultures lack – this isn't a competition. Rather, it's an attempt to identify the main ingredients in the European model itself. So here, to begin with, is an enumeration, in no particular order:

Rationality. Its presence at the head of the list doesn't in the slightest mean that Europeans are always reasonable, or that in their view reason should always be preferred to the passions or to intuition, but that the European tradition accepts the possibility of a rational knowledge of the world: the craziest actions, the most mysterious phenomena, can be apprehended by reason. And human affairs in their turn lend themselves to rational examination and to debate – which makes it possible for us to exchange arguments rather than blows. Reason is capable of knowing and understanding. The postulate of rationality is a necessary (but not sufficient) premise for the rise of both science and democracy. It is opposed to obscurantism, to superstition, to magical thinking, to sleight of hand.

This postulate goes back at least as far as pre-Socratic Greece, and, in the form of respect for science as well as for argued political debate, it extends right through Western history. Perhaps this long tradition is the reason why, in the twentieth century, Europeans became aware of a particular perversion of this way of thinking that occurs when it ceases to be a tool of knowledge and understanding and becomes instead the ultimate justification for our acts. At least since the bombing of Hiroshima, we know all too well that the labors of science are not entirely positive, and that reason is an instrument that doesn't guarantee the moral quality of its results. Left to themselves, science and technology know no limits: in a world where they rule alone, once a thing is possible, it becomes obligatory. So Europeans have realized that ultimate choices must not depend directly on objective knowledge, and cannot be decided by an impartial reason. They reject scientism: they want action to be guided by politics or morality, in other words by their will, their desires, their ideals – not by knowledge. But they refuse to fall into the other extreme and to see in science a threat rather than a promise; and even less will they renounce the principle of rationality.

Justice. Again, it is in ancient Greece that we find the first attempts to defend the principle of justice in Europe. Living in cities as they do, men realize that they have every interest in subjecting the life of the community to laws rather than leaving it prey solely to conflicts of will against will. Since it is they themselves who decide on the law, even if they are subject to it, they are not losing their freedom: they are submitting to their own will, and this autonomy allows them to find fulfillment. Behind particular laws there appears the idea of justice: what would be the right thing to do if we were to put aside our own interests – and thus, what would be the right thing for all, universally? The just order is intangible, it goes beyond everything that exists, beyond individuals' desires. "The pleasant is distinct from the good," says Socrates (*Gorgias* 500d),[2] and the just is on the side of the good: it is as it is, not because it gives me pleasure, but because it could satisfy everyone, so long as everyone abstains from judging in virtue of his own desires and interests.

Justice is opposed to egotism, to the demand for privileges and advantages – which one can, conversely, obtain by resorting to force. Socrates' antagonist, in the *Republic*, affirms, " 'Right' is always the same, the interest of the stronger party."[3] And his lesson has not been forgotten. The neo-fundamentalist ideologue, Gary Schmitt, declares, for example, "The United States has the right to be the 'major arbiter' in security affairs because it is the only civilized power which has the ability and the will to do what is necessary to prevent uncivilized countries from undermining peace and security."[4] However we define "civilized" in this sentence, it's not enough to convert might, even the greatest might, into right.

In order to act, justice cannot do without force. The idea of the just is embodied in universal principles, in natural law, in human rights, then in constitutions and positive law; but in order to be applied, these laws must be backed by state force. Nonetheless, the state doesn't have a right to do anything and everything: it is in turn required to respect the law. That is why governments are not authorized to practice torture, even against their worst enemies, nor to hold them illegally, like the ghosts of Guantánamo.

It is also in the name of justice that Europeans refuse to be governed merely by economic forces. In Communist countries, the economy was subject to politics and, as a result, withered. But nor is there any reason why politics should in every respect obey the economy ("market laws"): the economic dynamic must be able to operate, but states such as the European Union endeavor to limit and correct its effects in the name of social justice, in other words the protection of the weakest (not a mechanical redistribution of wealth but an institutionalized solidarity).

On the international level, Europeans again legitimate power by the way it is exercised, and of their own will impose limits on it, constraining themselves by treaties and contracts, and setting up institutions common to all. Such is the principle that lies at the basis of "tranquil force."

Democracy. Another Greek invention, one which wants power to be in the hands of the "people," in other words, all citizens. Everyone knows that this excluded a great number of people from Greek citizenship (women, slaves, men of foreign origin); modern democracy no longer rejects anyone apart from madmen and criminals (and children). Our democratic participation takes the form of a vote, in which we elect our representatives for a certain time; and since each and every one is a member of the "people" to the same degree, our rights are strictly identical, and every vote counts for as much as every other. A state which infringes in any way whatsoever this principle of absolute equality before the law can thus not be called a democracy. Thus South Africa at the time of apartheid was clearly not a democracy; but neither was the United States before the abolition of all racial discrimination (hence the struggle for civil rights). Likewise, any state which grants certain of its citizens specific rights in accordance with their religion, language, or customs is not a democracy. Democracy is not a "natural" political state, in the sense that it demands that all citizens belong to a particular category (race, religion, etc.), but a "contractual" state.

A state can conform to the spirit of justice without being a democracy; however, European peoples are attached to the idea of a democratic regime.

Individual freedom. The individual acquires a status in Greece, because it is the individual who has access to reason (given to each and every person), benefits from justice (universal but experienced at first hand by everyone), and participates in democracy (he can put his wishes into practice). The formula "man is the measure of all things" also requires that we judge the usefulness of actions in relation to the benefits that the individual receives from them, even if the interests of the community, or those of humanity as a whole, are not left out of the picture. But it is the Christian religion which gives a decisive impetus to this notion, since, unlike previous doctrines, it affirms the direct relation between God and each man. This relation, admittedly, does not extend to every aspect of human life, simply to those which affect its creator; but the value of the individual will become ever more strongly established in the social world of men and women.

Now one feature of the individual will here play an essential role: his liberty, understood as a capacity to act in accordance with his own will. The lack of liberty may be of two kinds. *Either* men are entirely determined by their nature (or, as people used to put it, by their race, their blood; these days they say their genes), or else by their culture (language, religion, education); in this case it would be better to entrust science with the reins of their behavior, rather than let them wander around at a loss. *Or* they are subject to the control of other individuals, or institutions, or the State; in an extreme case, the individual is reduced to slavery. So it's the possibility of escaping these two constraints, the one impersonal, the other social, which circumscribes the liberty of the individual: man, said Rousseau, can in all circumstances "acquiesce or resist."[5]

For this reason, Europeans cherish the regimes that respect their right to liberty; this is what they call a "liberal

democracy." Democracy alone, indeed, is not enough for
them: the people might decide that they need to impose
the Terror, or cannibalism, or the extermination of the
weakest members in the group; the individual would have
no right to protest if his liberty were not at the same time
protected. Every man and every woman has the right not
to follow the group's prescriptions without incurring any
punishment, so long as his liberty does not directly harm
others: this restrictive formula leaves room for debate, and
enables one to understand that for certain people, women
without a veil are a public nuisance, while for others por-
nography on television is not. So the consensus can evolve;
but all Europeans agree in demanding liberty of belief,
liberty of opinion, and liberty in the way we organize our
private lives; and they also agree in refusing to allow the
State to constrain individuals by force, as totalitarian
regimes did. The right to belong to a minority (linguistic,
religious, or other) without being subjected to persecution
is part and parcel of these individual liberties.

By postulating the liberty of the individual vis-à-vis the
causes that condition him, we simultaneously affirm that
each person remains, until his dying day, an unfinished
being; he is perfectible, he can change (for better or worse).
This is one of the reasons why the European Union demands that all its members renounce the death penalty,
which denies the criminal the possibility of changing, and
thus refuses to allow him to belong to the human race –
which is, in its turn, a form of crime.

Secularism. Paradoxically, the idea of secularism comes
from a religious tradition: Christianity. By saying "Render
therefore unto Caesar the things which are Caesar's; and
unto God the things that are God's" (Matthew 22: 21),
and "My Kingdom is not of this world" (John 18: 36),
Christ imposed a radical separation between Heaven and
Earth, between the theological realm and the political.
Secularism designates, not the absence of the religious or
its rejection, but this same separation, and thus the refusal

to impose Christian values by the sword. Despite Christ's original formulation, the separation did not happen without great difficulty, even at the very heart of the Christian tradition. When Christianity became the official religion of a State, there was a great temptation to base the laws of the city of men on those of the city of God and to submit royal power to the authority of the head of the Church, the Pope. Only in the fourteenth century, with its armed conflicts between popes and emperors, did we see the first great theorists of secularism, Marsilius of Padua and William of Occam, set out the theoretical foundations of the sovereign State, as well as the parallel separation between faith and reason.

The opposite of secularism is ideocracy, i.e. the confusion between ideology and State. Ideocracy may take the form of a theocracy, with the clergy deciding on the political decisions people make; but also – and it was in this guise that the threat became concrete in the twentieth century in Europe – that of totalitarianism, when the Party, the bearer of ideology, became indistinguishable from the State. The traumatic experience of Communism and Nazism has made Europeans particularly vigilant towards any infringement of secularism. It is also probably the part of the world where religious practices are most strictly reserved to the private sphere.

This choice has an important consequence. Since Heaven and Earth are separated, any attempt to establish an earthly paradise is banned. Contemporary secular states do not purport to ensure the definitive triumph of the values they defend, nor to cure humanity of its defects once and for all. Man is resolutely imperfect, his societies are subject to criticism, and will always be so. Europeans today re-encounter, but in a quite different form, the Christian idea of original sin, that cannot be wiped out in this life. Conversely, they oppose any millenarian or messianic heresy that would seek to build the heavenly kingdom here and now. They refuse, for this reason, to accept the downgrading of the present in favor of some glorious future.

Tolerance. Tolerance, another heritage from religious history, is today understood in a broader sense. It starts out from a simple observation – that of the extraordinary diversity between men and between societies; and it posits a separation between the differences that are tolerable and those that are not. What is intolerable, within a State, is punished by law – offenses and crimes, violence itself as it serves intolerance. This leaves aside the vast domain of tolerable differences. Neither individuals nor groups are obliged to approve of other people's ways of thinking and acting; but they do not have any right to prevent them persisting in their choices or to persecute them.

Europe presents the picture of an extraordinary assemblage of differences. To the plurality of languages we can add that of customs, traditions, ways of organizing time and space (both public and private), social groups, professions, and parties. The smallness of states made relations between them inevitable. After having waged war on each other for centuries, after subjecting each other to mutual hatred and contempt, the peoples of Europe have finally managed to live together within a single union. The differences have not vanished as if by magic, but they have ceased to be a source of hostility and can even be appreciated for what they are. As Jacques Derrida and Jürgen Habermas have commented, "the recognition of differences – the mutual recognition of the other for his alterity – can also become the mark of a common identity."[6]

We might wonder in this context whether the unification of Europe, which, furthermore, has come about in the age of globalization, doesn't threaten this cultural diversity. For my part, I believe the danger to be exaggerated. Human beings have always been able to draw a distinction between civic (or administrative) identity and cultural identity; in this regard, the nation-state is rather the exception than the rule. Possessing a European passport doesn't in the slightest stop you feeling Spanish at heart, and even Andalusian. And these cultural identities are less fragile than they are made out to be. Admittedly, certain minority languages are dying out; but so long as they are spoken by at least a few million people, they hold up well. The population of Bulgaria, including all the minorities, is less than ten million strong; I have yet to hear that Bulgarian children are these days starting to speak English, German, or Russian. The "Europe" effect would mean rather that Bulgarian children, knowing that their mother tongue is little spoken outside their country's borders, soon start learning foreign languages. French and German people find the same products in their supermarkets, but their languages still remain just as impermeable to one another as before. When two nationals from these countries meet, there's a good chance they'll talk to each other in "international English"; but at home, each of them speaks his native tongue. And it isn't just a question of language: you can recognize a French or German person from the way they cross the road, or bring up their children, or participate in the intellectual life of their country: traditions are long-lasting.

Why does European integration change nothing, or hardly anything? The reason is that these traditions are not transmitted simultaneously, between people of the same generation, but successively, from one generation to another. Languages evolve, of course, but very slowly; we can still understand the sixteenth-century French of Montaigne. The way we imagine our world is, in this regard, misleading: the link between the generations is generally underestimated, since we always like to think of ourselves as free subjects, making up our own minds from a *tabula rasa*. Culture is part of this transmission from one generation to the next, and for this reason it easily resists unification.

Military power – however "tranquil" – means soldiers who accept putting their lives in danger. But no one is willing to die so that import duties will fall, or the Dow Jones rise. National states themselves no longer arouse much emotional support: we content ourselves with asking them to provide us with services. The defense of European identity and the values that go to make it up is a better justification for the risks involved by taking charge of our own defense for ourselves. So long as Europe is no more than a commodity, it cannot arouse any passion; for that to happen, it must also be an idea.

— 8 —

Adapting Institutions

If we adopt the vision of Europe sketched out in the preceding pages, it's easy to see that European institutions, as they exist here and now, do not serve it well; so they ought to be transformed. Indeed, various different assemblies have been devoting themselves to this end, especially the European Convention in 2003. I would like to take advantage of the fact that I don't belong to any commission, and answer to no one, to reflect at full liberty on the institutions that would be most appropriate for a new Europe. I will make my task much easier by limiting myself to asking about only what is desirable, without bothering about how it might be realized. But in my view, before we seek the means, we need to agree on the end.

The suggestions that follow do not have the merit of originality; they have been formulated by other writers, from a wide range of political backgrounds whether "Left" or "Right." But that's just the point: there are many suggestions going the rounds, and they are often mutually incompatible. Rather than any originality, what I seek is consistency: supposing we agree on the spirit of a future Europe, what institutions would suit it best?

I have spoken of the necessity for Europe to assume its role as a "tranquil power" – in other words, as an autonomous military force, capable of defending itself against any adversary (other than the United States), as well as aiding its allies. This transformation demands a pooling of, and a significant increase in, military budgets.

Once this force has been constituted, the question of its relations with NATO immediately raises its head. NATO should in its turn transform itself in two ways. On the one hand, by becoming autonomous in the military sphere, Europe should take back its equipment from NATO and place it under its own control. On the other hand, a greatly restricted NATO would still be useful as a frame for military cooperation between the European Union and the United States, in situations in which such cooperation becomes necessary (solidarity in the case of aggression against one of the partners, the struggle against Islamic terrorism, etc.).

Not all countries in the European Union are ready to abandon NATO and replace it by a European force. This is especially so in the case of East European countries, who still live with the painful memory of Soviet interventionism: in their view, American protection is more reliable than European protection. It is neither a good thing nor even possible to force them; it is only with time that they may change their minds. For that to happen, the trauma of totalitarianism must fade away, on the one hand; and the European army must increase in power, on the other. A day will come when these countries will judge that it is in their interests to join a European force; then they will do it willingly.

The case of Great Britain is different because, for numerous reasons, it has linked its military policy to that of the United States. Here too, we will need to wait for change to come from within: Great Britain might find it advantageous to play the master on this side of the Atlantic rather than the servant on the other. This change is all the more desirable in that the British army is the biggest in Europe;

it is indeed to the British army that leadership of the future defense of the Union should be entrusted.

Meanwhile, we must thus start with the realization that not all the countries of Europe aspire in the same way to military integration. Rather than passively awaiting the change, as several observers have remarked, a new approach is necessary: we should set up, not a multi-speed Europe, but one consisting of several concentric circles.

The inner circle, or kernel, would be made up of the countries that accept this fact: the problems of security and of relations with non-European countries are things they all share, since no danger threatens them from within Europe. At the same time, acting in self-defense together and acting outside Europe together are preferable: their intervention would then carry more weight. So these countries would decide to unify their foreign policies as well as their defense policies. Such a community is no longer a confederation, or an association of independent states, as is currently the case of the Union, but a federation. It seems that the founding states of the Union – Germany, Benelux, France, Italy – would agree on taking this step; so they could found, within the Union itself, a European Federation.

One consequence of this measure would be that the French President would find himself stripped of what is called his "reserved domain," i.e. defense and foreign affairs. So French institutions would be led to evolve towards a more directly parliamentary regime.

The next concentric circle would be that of the European Union in its current form: soon to be a set of 25 countries and, in a relatively short time, 35 (including the Balkan countries, Moldavia, and Norway). The criteria for belonging to this circle are well known: a certain level of economic development, juridical guarantees, a political regime of liberal democracy. Each new member will have to conform to essential European values, like those enumerated here. We know that this demand is already responsible for encouraging transformations in a country such as Turkey: the suspension of the death penalty, the recognition of minority rights. The fact that the majority religion in one of these countries is Islam is no obstacle; what counts these days in Europe is not Christianity, but one of its paradoxical heritages: secularism.

The European Union would thus be a unified space for the economy, justice and the police, culture and education. Its members could one day join the Federation, or they could stay outside.

A third circle would extend beyond this. Europe cannot exist if it has no frontiers, within which a certain consensus can be established. But where will they be set? The states that constitute Europe must remain comparable in size. That is why Russia will never form part of the Union, however close its culture may be to that of other European countries, and also whatever political regime it may have: the country is too huge, its population too great, and its inclusion would have a destabilizing effect. The case of Ukraine and Byelorussia is rather different, since they are states of smaller size, and one day they will need to choose between a closer union with Russia or integration into the European Union. For the same reason, the countries of the Maghreb are not destined to form part of it: taken together, they represent too large an area, and there would be no reason to stop at Morocco or Algeria, etc.

But Europe cannot, for all that, ignore those countries, which are destined to be its main zones of influence. Relations of many kinds, both institutional and human, exist already; they will grow stronger, since they will profit all parties. Europe cannot be cut of from its south and its east, where in any case the geographical frontiers are easy to cross; populations, resources, and needs are complementary on both sides. For historical and geographical reasons, it is probable that certain European countries will favor exchanges with the rest of the Mediterranean, and others with the east of the continent; both are necessary to Europe.

Such a restructuring of Europe in three circles simultaneously implies that its central institutions be reinforced.

First of all, they need to become more democratic, in other words reflect the European population rather than just the states within it – since the aim of the Union, after all, is to absorb states and go beyond them. The current principle dictating that, on various levels, every state has just as much power as every other, is absurd. It recalls the exorbitant privileges enjoyed by certain groups under the ancien régime. The French Revolution took a great step, on the night of 4 August 1789, when it abolished privileges; it is time that the European Union enact its own 4 August. The way things are now, the six most populous countries of the Union comprise 70 percent of the population, and yet they carry the same weight – as they do in the Commission – as the six least populous countries, whose population does not even amount to 1 percent of the population. This situation is all the more unacceptable when a unified military force needs to be created: an army implies a budget, soldiers, and means – all in proportion to the population. It is unacceptable, in this context, for Malta to count as much as Italy. If the terms of the contract are clearly formulated in advance, the populations in these different countries will not demur at these renunciations. After all, we are ready to admit, within each country, that a single party governs the affairs of state – even when we had voted for the opposite party.

The most democratic institution in Europe is its parliament – a direct expression of the peoples of Europe. This correlation must be made even stronger, by insisting on proportional representation: by establishing, for instance, the principle that one deputy be elected per million of the population. A clear and simple idea, which anyone can understand. Within each country, the ballot would remain proportional by list, which would ensure the representation of all main tendencies.

On the other hand, the leadership of the Union should be reinforced by giving it the legitimacy of suffrage: we need to elect a president of Europe. But direct suffrage is not suitable here: politicians are not well known outside their own country, and each people may well simply vote for its own national. We could get round this problem, however, if the president of Europe were elected by the MEPs – it would be their first task – for the same length of time and in the same conditions as the deputies themselves. This election by parliament, perfectly democratic, would have the advantage of counterbalancing national affinities by enabling people to take up positions on the big political choices. French socialists would probably prefer to vote for a German socialist candidate rather than a French right-winger. So this president would be representative of the parliamentary majority and would himself be one of the deputies, which would allow him to be both well known in his own country (where he would lead one of the big lists for election to the European Parliament) and familiar with affairs on the broader scale.

The president of Europe would have the authority to set out the main lines of European policy. He would be assisted in his work by, on the one hand, the Minister(s) of Defense and Foreign Affairs of the European Federation and, on the other hand, by the Commission of which he would be the head. The "commissioners" of this body would no longer represent the member states, but would be appointed by the president for their personal qualities and competencies, since it would be their task to safeguard the well-being of Europe as a whole, not that of the countries they come from. These countries, conversely, would send their representatives (one per country, for instance their ministers of European Affairs) to a Council that would exercise a role of surveillance.

The Convention for the Future of Europe, presided over by Valéry Giscard d'Estaing, has just published its planned Constitution, which concerns European institutions. Certain of its recommendations concur with those suggested here: a Europe capable of its own defense, bringing together just a few states (the future Federation), is made possible; the president of the Commission will indeed be elected by the Parliament. Unfortunately, a number of concessions had to be made to national governments, who refuse to let go of a scrap of their power: so the preponderant role of the Council, as a direct expression of individual states, is preserved, as is that of its president; commissioners, i.e. European ministers, are chosen in virtue of their national origin, instead of on the sole criterion of their individual qualities. Doubtless it was impossible to go any further towards integration. The fact remains that the very existence of a European Constitution is a major step: the Union can proclaim its identity of spirit in it, and not merely its identity of economic interests.

If the European Union had a president endowed with powers, it would become a much more effective institution than it is today. Another transformation would also help it along this path: adopting a single working language. The suggestion risks incurring the displeasure of all nationalists, and yet it's a matter of common sense. In any case, it's hardly a radical innovation: in the Middle Ages, a Europe of the élites existed, thanks, above all, to the possibility of communication across borders in Latin. Today only one language can play this role: the language I call "international English." It's not the language of Shakespeare or Henry James. It's the language spoken by all Europeans when they want to make themselves understood when they travel to most parts of the world outside their own. It's the language used amongst themselves by scientists from every country if they want to find out how their discipline is developing. It's the language in which the young people of a neighboring country communicate when they travel to neighboring countries. I even suspect that it's the language which European bureaucrats use once the microphones are switched off. We need to have the courage to admit what is simply a matter of fact.

The existence of this auxiliary international language doesn't threaten national cultures or languages in their many and various functions. All due respect to the French! Born into the Bulgarian language, I made the personal choice to express myself in French, and I don't regret that for a minute. But I also know that a mode of expression is one thing, and the functioning of an institution such as the European Union, quite another. To learn international English, these days, ought to be as automatic as learning to drive a car or use a computer. To be able to enter into direct contact with foreigners is a wonderful advantage, since it enables everyone to take up a certain distance vis-à-vis himself or herself, to distinguish between the natural and the conventional aspects of his or her own behavior, and to enable his or her thoughts to reach out to those of others. Once this initial contact has been established, the way is open to knowing other cultures as well as other languages.

I have one last suggestion to make, a much less controversial one, and easier to realize. We need to establish in Europe a holiday, a celebration for Europe, in which we would celebrate its coming into being. There's already an obvious suitable date: 8 (or 9) May, the day on which the Second World War ended. Germany, vanquished in this war, has no less reason than other countries to celebrate this date; her defeat was also a victory for her, since it freed her from Nazism and enabled her to become a founding member of the new Europe. The European Union is the indirect, yet logical outcome of this conflict and its ending; but it is also a project for the future. And so, rather than merely commemorating the past on this date, we would recognize in it the basis for our current actions.

May–June 2003

Notes

Chapter 1 The Reasons for the War

1 <http://www.sacbee.com/24hour/front/story/811657p-5767549c.html>, accessed 1 March 2004.
2 <http://www.presidentialrhetoric.com/speeches/02.26.03.html>, accessed 1 March 2004.
3 Ibid.
4 Ibid.
5 Robert Kagan, *Of Paradise and Power: America and Europe in the New World Order* (New York: Knopf, 2003), p. 41.

Chapter 2 The Neo-fundamentalists

1 G. F. Kennan, "The Sources of Soviet Conduct," *Foreign Affairs*, July 1947, repr. in James F. Hoge Jr and Fareed Zakaria (eds), *The American Encounter: The United States and the Making of the Modern World* (New York: Basic Books, 1997), p. 169.
2 <http://www.globalsecurity.org/military/library/policy/national/nss-020920.pdf>, accessed 1 March 2004.
3 <http://opinionjournal.com/ac/?id=110002988>, accessed 1 March 2004.

4 Vasilii Grossman, *Life and Fate*, tr. Robert Chandler (New York: Harper & Row, 1985), new edn (London: Harvill, 1995), p. 406.

Chapter 3   The Fragility of the Empire

1 Raymond Aron, *Études politiques* (Paris: Gallimard, 1972), p. 506.
2 <http://www.commondreams.org/views03/0121-07.htm>, accessed 1 March 2004.
3 *Courier international*, 25 April 2003.
4 General Wesley K. Clark, *Waging Modern War: Bosnia, Kosovo, and the Future of Combat* (Oxford: Perseus, 2001), p. 430.
5 *Le Monde*, 16 April 2003.
6 Don Van Natta Jr, "Questioning Terror Suspects in a Dark and Surreal World," *New York Times*, 9 March 2003; <http://www.globalpolicy.org/wtc/liberties/2003/0309questioning.htm>, accessed 1 March 2004.
7 Ibid.

Chapter 4   In Praise of Pluralism

1 Aron, *Études*, p. 509.
2 <http://www.ambafrance-au.org/media/pages/s2003/s3203.en.htm>, accessed 1 March 2004.
3 Charles de Montesquieu, *Persian Letters*, tr. C. J. Betts (Harmondsworth: Penguin, 1973), p. 191.
4 <http://globalsecurity.org/military/library/policy/national/nss-020920.pdf>, accessed 1 March 2004.
5 Plato, *Republic*, tr. Desmond Lee, 2nd rev. edn (Harmondsworth: Penguin, 1987), 360c (p. 47).
6 Immanuel Kant, "To Perpetual Peace: A Philosophical Sketch" (1795), in *Perpetual Peace and Other Essays*, tr. Ted Humphrey (Indianapolis and Cambridge: Hackett, 1983), p. 125.

Chapter 5   Might or Right?

1 <http://www.ambafrance-au.org/media/pages/s2003/home.en.htm>, accessed 1 March 2004.
2 Ibid.
3 Ibid.
4 Ibid.
5 Interview with *Le Monde*, 13 May 2003.
6 Jean-Jacques Rousseau, "Que l'état de guerre naît de l'état social," in *Oeuvres complètes*, vol. 3 (Paris: Gallimard-Pléiade, 1975), p. 610.
7 Raymond Aron, *Paix et guerre entre les nations* (Paris: Calmann-Lévy, 1962), p. 721.
8 *Le Monde des débats*, 25 May 2001.
9 Cf. Paul Hazan, *La Justice face à la guerre: de Nuremberg à La Haye* (Paris: Stock, 2000), p. 219.

Chapter 6   A Tranquil Power

1 *Le Monde*, 5 April 2003.
2 *International Herald Tribune*, 24 January 2003.
3 *Le Monde*, 23–24 March 2003.

Chapter 7   European Values

1 Jean-Jacques Rousseau, "Extrait du projet de paix perpétuelle," in *Oeuvres complètes*, vol. 3, p. 565.
2 Plato, *Gorgias*, 500d.
3 Plato, *The Republic*, 339a; *The Republic*, 2nd rev. edn, tr. Desmond Lee (Harmondsworth: Penguin, 1974), p. 20.
4 *Le Monde*, 23–24 March 2003.
5 Jean-Jacques Rousseau, "Discourse on the origin of inequality," in *The Discourses and Other Early Political Writings*, ed. and tr. Victor Gourevitch (Cambridge: Cambridge University Press, 1997), p. 141.
6 *Libération*, 31 May 2003. Eng. tr. <http://watch.windsof change.net/themes_63.htm>, accessed 15 July 2004.

Index

311